PUBLISHER'S NOTE

—

Citadel Pioneer Books are devoted to telling the story of the American frontier, and the life of the men and women who were the pioneers in shaping the American West. These are the intimate memoirs, journals, autobiographies and other writings that provide the basic source material for an understanding of the rise of the American Nation. For, basically, the story of the expanding frontier is the story of the United States.

THE WESTERN COUNTRY
Drawn by Russell Martin to illustrate the Memoirs of Cadillac and Liette

THE WESTERN COUNTRY IN THE 17th CENTURY

The memoirs of Antoine Lamothe Cadillac and Pierre Liette

A CITADEL PIONEER BOOK

THE CITADEL PRESS / NEW YORK

EDITED BY

MILO MILTON QUAIFE

Historical Introduction

WHEN the white man came to America he found the continent everywhere occupied by a copper-hued race of men upon whom the mistaken geographical ideas of Columbus has fixed the name of Indians. Although to the new comers all Indians looked pretty much alike, in fact the scores of tribes scattered over the continent were keenly aware of their separate identities and they exhibited a culture ranging upward from the way of life of the Digger Indians of the Great Basin to that of the relatively civilized Aztecs of Mexico.

Most of the tribes inhabiting the Great Lakes and the upper Mississippi Valley belonged to the Algonquian linguistic family and had developed a semi-hunting, semi-agricultural economy and culture. They had become a sedentary people, fiercely devoted to their homeland and the graves of their ancestors. They had made respectable progress in the realm of agriculture, raising crops of corn, tobacco, pumpkins, melons, and other vegetables, but none in animal husbandry. Their habitations were crude, usually consisting of a framework of poles or branches covered over with skins or mats made of reeds, and readily taken down for removal to another site or abandoned altogether. They built no bridges or improved highways, and save for the numerous ceremonial and other mounds, no permanent structures of any kind.

Since they knew nothing of individual ownership of the land and possessed but a scanty store of personal property their social life exhibited a high degree of communism. They were highly hospitable, sharing their cabins and food, and even their wives and daughters with the stranger in their midst. Their governmental ideas were no less rudimentary. The chiefs, or leaders, had but little real authority over their followers, and because of certain conceptions of the obligations of clanship and of the attainment of manhood, warfare was a perennial occupation. War and the chase, in fact, were practically the sole occupations of the men, and he who was most skillful in these pursuits commanded the highest esteem of his fellows.

To the wondering eyes of the red man the European newcomer exhibited a bewildering array of treasures. Above all else he brought guns and other iron implements—hatchets, knives, traps and many more—so vastly superior to the Indian's stone-age implements that at first contact he thought their white possessors must be gods. Before me as I write are two tools, a clumsy stone knife or skinner, and a marvellously light and efficient penknife. The contrast between them illustrates vividly the gulf which separated primitive man from his more fortunate Iron-age successor.

As soon as the Indian became aware of the existence of these marvelous implements he conceived an urgent desire to possess them. But the white trader was no philanthropist, and practically the only product the Indian could offer in exchange for the goods he desired was the skins of the wild animals that crowded the American wilderness. Here in a nutshell we have the basis of the fur trade, whose pursuit led Old-World monarchs to engage in deadly wars, and went far to shape the history of North America.

Almost at a single bound the Indian passed from the Stone to the Iron Age. So quickly was the change effected, in fact, that only the earlier white visitors encountered him while he still remained in his primitive state. The white trader commonly lacked either a motive or the ability to record his observations of the native way of life for the enlightenment of future generations, and so we are heavily indebted to the reports of the Jesuit and other missionaries for much of our knowledge of the primitive Indian culture. Fortunately, however, a few traders and officials also recorded their observations, and two of the best of these Memoirs are presented to the reader of the present book.

The one written by Antoine Lamothe Cadillac was designed by its author as a comprehensive picture of the life of the tribes of the Upper Country, as the French called the region of the Great Lakes and the upper Mississippi Valley; the narrative of Pierre Liette, on the other hand, is devoted to a detailed and specific description of the Illinois Indians alone. Thus, although the two authors cover common ground to considerable extent, their narratives admirably complement each other. Both narratives belong to the closing years of the seventeenth century, and the observations of both writers were made at a time when the western Indians still retained, for the most part, their primitive way of life.

Antoine Lamothe Cadillac was one of the brilliant lieutenants whom Governor Frontenac recruited to save New France from impending destruction in the desperate war of 1690–97. Its opening act disclosed an invading English-Colonial fleet and army sum-

moning Quebec itself to surrender, while the
many tribes of the Upper Country, long the
allies of the French, were disheartened by the
blows already dealt New France by the rav-
aging Iroquois, and were wavering in their
allegiance to their French "father."

Although Frontenac's situation at Quebec
was desperate enough, he clearly saw the
necessity of retaining their allegiance at any
cost, and dispatched a body of soldiery to
Mackinac, where Fort de Buade had been
established on the site of present-day St.
Ignace. It became at once the chief post of
the western country and the center upon
which all the others were dependent. To it
Cadillac was sent as commandant in 1694.
In 1696 the King was persuaded by his ad-
visers to issue an order requiring the with-
drawal of all the garrisons from the Upper
Country, and the return of all Frenchmen
save the missionaries to Lower Canada.

Although the coureurs des bois snapped
their fingers at the royal decree, the officials
of the government must obey it. In 1697,
therefore, Fort de Buade was evacuated,
along with Fort St. Joseph at the southerly
end of Lake Michigan, and the garrisons
made the long journey back to Lower Canada.

The new policy constituted a crushing
blow to the welfare of the colony, and even-

tually it was completely reversed. Foremost in voicing this demand was Cadillac, who, following his return to Quebec, went to Paris to urge upon the King his project for the establishment of a fort and colony on the "strait," the waterway by which the waters of Lake Huron descend to Lake Erie. Such a post, he correctly argued, would serve as an effective check upon the Iroquois, and upon the entrance of the English to the Upper Lakes. In short, it would replace Mackinac as a new and better center of French control over all the Upper Country.

Cadillac's appeal was granted and he returned to America to lay the foundation of the city of Detroit in July, 1701. Ten years later he was summarily dismissed and ordered to a new station at Mobile in infant Louisiana. Although the builder departed in gloom and defeat his work of founding the future metropolis was accomplished; his infant wilderness capital has today become America's fourth city and perhaps the foremost industrial center of the earth.

The varying fortunes which befall lost manuscripts would afford material for an absorbing volume. When they are retained in private possession they are almost certain, sooner or later, to be destroyed or their value to become unknown and their whereabouts forgotten. Even when they are given over to the custody of a public institution, the hazards to which they are exposed, although lessened, are still far too common. The story of Cadillac's Memoir, as also of Liette's, will serve to illustrate these remarks.

In the summer of 1695 Cadillac wrote a letter from St. Ignace to Governor Frontenac at Quebec stating, among other things, that he was preparing a relation and a map of the Upper Country.[1] Both were eventually completed, as we know from the Memoir printed in the pages that follow this introductory note. That the Memoir was not completed until after the close of his command at Fort de Buade is evident from certain of its statements. The motive which inspired its preparation can only be inferred from our general knowledge of Cadillac's character and career. He was a fluent disputant and ready writer, who had evidently obtained in earlier life a fair education. Ambitious and enterprising, he was fertile in conceiving designs of statecraft and urging them upon his superiors for adoption. In 1693, for example, he prepared a project for ending the Iroquois-English menace to New France by the con-

[1]For this letter see Rev. Jean Delanglez, "Cadillac at Michilimackinac," in *Mid-America*, XXVII, 110 and 202.

quest of New York. More notable was his subsequent project, successfully urged upon the French Monarch and Ministry, for the founding of Detroit. Preparation of the Memoir and map of the Upper Country at least served to occupy a portion of his time while immersed in the western wilderness, and it may also have been motivated by a desire to attract the favorable attention of his governmental superiors. Whether or not it was actually utilized for this purpose we have no information.

Nor do we know anything of the fate of the map, which has now been lost to the world for two and a half centuries. As for the Memoir, the manuscript, or more probably a longhand copy of it, came into the hands of Pierre Margry two generations ago, who printed it in Volume V of his extensive collection of Memoirs and Documents dealing with the early explorations and settlements of the French in North America. Here it has been available to scholars, although practically unknown to the general public, for the last seventy years. The copy is dated January 31, 1718, which Margry notes was four months after Cadillac's release from the Bastille. At some date prior to 1911 Mr. Edward E. Ayer acquired a copy of the Memoir, which is now preserved in the Newberry Library at Chicago. Presumably this is the same copy as the one Margry used, but the Library has no record of its provenance prior to its acquisition by that institution. Presumably also the date placed at the conclusion of the manuscript indicates the day the copyist finished transcribing it; but neither of these presumptions is susceptible of proof.

It remains to account for our present translation of the Memoir. A generation ago Mr. Clarence M. Burton of Detroit, diligent collector of Detroit and Mid-western historical materials, undertook to have the contents of the entire Margry Collection published in English translation with a view to making them available to the general reader. To this end, he enlisted the cooperation of the great London bookseller, B. F. Stevens, who assigned the task of translation to his trusted long-time employee, Miss Edith Moodie, who compared the printed documents with their Paris originals, with a view to eliminating those errors which had gained entrance to Margry's published volumes. Both Mr. Burton and Miss Moodie have long since died. It is a pleasure here to acknowledge their scholarly zeal and to be instrumental, if only in a minor way, in putting into print one of the Memoirs Mr. Burton caused to be translated. It must be added,

however, that although I have utilized Miss
Moodie's translation, I have freely altered its
phraseology, chiefly with the aim of supply-
ing a less literal and more smoothly flowing
English version. If in the process I have in-
advertently perpetrated any errors, the responsibility for them rests upon me, and not
upon Miss Moodie.

It should be added, also, that I have had
no access to the copy of the Memoir in the
Ayer Collection, and hence have had no opportunity to check Miss Moodie's translation by comparison with it. Comparison has
been made, however, with the small portion
of the Memoir, translated from Margry,
which was published in Vol. XVI of the *Wisconsin Historical Collections*, and some of its
phraseology has been substituted for Miss
Moodie's translation.

Lorenzo de Tonty was a banker of Naples
who in 1647 participated in a popular insur-
rection against the Spanish viceroy. It failed
and as a consequence Lorenzo migrated to
France, where his eldest son, Henry, was
born about the year 1650. At the age of
eighteen he entered the French army, where
he served for a decade, until the Peace of
Nimwegen in 1678 left him without employ-

ment. Opportunely he was introduced to
Robert Cavalier, Sieur de La Salle, who was
in France recruiting aid for his projected ex-
ploration and colonization of the Mississippi
Valley. Tonty entered his service, and until
the death of La Salle in 1687 remained his
devoted and capable lieutenant and follower.
In partnership with La Forest, Tonty succeeded to La Salle's trading privilege in Illinois, continuing for many more years the
trading activities which the fallen leader had
initiated.

Henry Tonty had a younger brother, Alphonse, born in 1659, who also became an
army officer in New France. In 1701 he ac-
companied Cadillac to Detroit, as second in
command of this new post. Here he remained
until his death in 1727, being commandant of
Detroit during the last ten years of his life.

The mother of Henry and Alphonse was
Isabelle de Liette (in Italian, de Lietto),
and Pierre, a younger member of the family
clan, who may have been a cousin or a nephew
of Henry and Alphonse, was known by the
maternal family name throughout his life.
In 1687, while still quite young he followed
his kinsman to Illinois. For over forty years
thereafter he served either as trader or army
officer in the Mississippi Valley, chiefly
among the Illinois. He spent four years

among the Miami at Chicago (1698–1702)
and many more among the Illinois at Fort
St. Louis (Starved Rock) and Lake Peoria.
For a time he was commandant of the fort on
the Wabash, and for several years prior to his
death in 1729 he commanded the French post
in the Illinois.

Despite his long years of service and resi-
dence in the country, save for the facts per-
taining to his military service and for those
contained in his Memoir, printed in the present volume, we know but little about him.[2]
Presumably he was born in France, since the
remarkably well preserved vital records of
the Catholic Church in Quebec seem to con-
tain no mention of his baptism, nor of his
wife and children, if he had any.

The facts concerning his Memoir are similarly elusive. A generation or so ago Mr. Edward E. Ayer, whose notable historical collection is now the property of the Newberry
Library, obtained several bound volumes of
longhand transcripts of memoirs and narra-

[2]For the career of Henry De Tonty see sketch in
Dictionary of American Biography and references ap-
pended thereto. Benjamin Sulte, *"Les Tonty,"* in Royal
Soc. of Canada, *Proceedings* for 1893 (Vol. XI) 3–31,
supplies much information about the several members
of the Tonty family. For the Illinois career of Liette
see C. W. Alvord, *Illinois Country,* 1673–1818 (Spring-
field, 1918).

tives of discovery and allied subjects, which apparently had been made by some eighteenth-century copyist. Among the documents contained in the collection is the Memoir of Liette. What became of the original manuscript, we have no information. But the Memoir speaks for itself as by far the best depiction of Illinois and of its native inhabitants at the close of the seventeenth century ever penned.

Its closing lines propound a problem which we are unable to solve. "I desire with all my heart, Monsieur, that this memorial may give you pleasure, and prove worthy of your curiosity.

Montreal, Canada, October 20, 1721.

Signed: De Gannes."

But to whom were these lines addressed, and why the signature, "De Gannes" and the date, 1721? The Memoir itself discloses (*post*, 110) that it was written in 1702, at the close of Liette's four-year sojourn at Chicago. He lived until 1729, and as an army officer and as commandant of western posts he must have been well-known at Quebec, at least in official circles. The suggestion which has been advanced that the copyist was claiming the authorship of the Memoir is therefore incredible. Entirely plausible, however, is the assumption that his unidentified correspondent was aware of the relationship both of Liette as author and of De Gannes as copyist to the document.

As for De Gannes, this was the name of a family line long prominent and numerously represented in Canada, and many of those who bore it served as officers in the army. We have no means of identifying the one who signed Liette's Memoir, nor do we know of any connection between the De Gannes and the Tonty-Liette family groups.[3]

However these facts may be, the publication of Liette's Memoir fulfills an ambition conceived by the present writer some thirty years ago. Recognizing its historical interest and value I then obtained the permission of the Librarian of the Newberry Library to publish it, and enlisted the service of Dr. William F. Giese of the University of Wisconsin to translate it into English. The years passed, however, without my finding a suitable opportunity to publish the Memoir, and when Prof. Theodore C. Pease, Editor of the *Illinois Historical Collections*, asked permis-

[3] For the history of the several branches of the De Gannes family see Aegidius Fauteux, *"La Famille De Gannes,"* in *Bulletin Recherches Historiques*, XXXI, 271–85 and 331–41.

sion to include it in the first volume of *The French Foundations* series I reluctantly abandoned my long-delayed design of publishing it and transferred to him the translation Professor Giese had made.

So the Memoir was published in Volume XXIII of the *Illinois Historical Collections* in 1934, entitled "Memoir of De Gannes Concerning the Illinois Country." It has seemed to me, in preparing the present printing, to be more appropriate to credit it to Liette, whom we know in fact was its author. For the present translation, too, I must assume a major share of responsibility. Basically it is the Giese translation of thirty years ago, as modified by Professor Pease and his editorial helpers. But neither of these scholars seems to have been greatly concerned about the literary style of their respective versions. While utilizing these to the fullest practicable extent, I have endeavored to transpose the original narrative into as presentable English as possible. The changes of meaning from the two earlier translations are comparatively few; those of phraseology and literary composition are exceedingly abundant.

It remains to acknowledge the service of the Burton Historical Collection of the Detroit Public Library and of the Newberry Library, whose resources I have freely utilized; in particular the long-ago labor of Mr. Clarence M. Burton in procuring the translation of the Memoir of Cadillac, and the permission long since granted by the former Librarian of the Newberry and renewed by Dr. Pargellis, his present successor, to publish the Memoir of Liette. In like manner, Mr. Jay Monaghan, Editor of the Collections of the Illinois State Historical Library, has permitted me to utilize the earlier printing of Liette's Memoir edited by Professor Theodore C. Pease. Mr. Antoine Roy, Provincial Archivist of Quebec kindly supplied me with information concerning the Tonty and the De Gannes families of New France. Mr. Russell Martin of Detroit prepared the map drawn to illustrate the memoirs, while Mrs. Dorothy Martin patiently deciphered my deplorable penmanship and competently typed my editorial copy.

M. M. QUAIFE
Detroit, Michigan

Contents

Account

by the Sieur de Lamothe Cadillac,
Captain of Infantry in command of a company
of the troops of the Marine in Canada,
formerly Commandant of Michilimackinac
and other posts in the Upper Country, where
he remained for three years.

The Memoir of
Lamothe Cadillac

—

Chapter 1

THE word Michilimackinac means "Island of the Turtle." The reason why it is so called may be either because it is shaped like a turtle, or because one was found in the vicinity. It is in Lake Huron, and is nearly two leagues in circumference; it is a league and a half from the inhabited mainland; it is frequented only in the fishing season, when there is excellent fishing all round there.

Opposite the island is a large sandy cove, and it is here the French fort is situated, where there is a garrison and the commander-in-chief of the district resides, who has under him the commandants of the various posts; but both he and they are appointed by the Governor-General of New France. This post is called Fort de Buade.[1]

[1]For an account of the establishment of Fort de Buade on the site of present-day St. Ignace and a pic-

3

The Jesuit mission, the French village, and the villages of the Huron and Ottawa are adjacent to one another, and together they border and fill up the head of the cove. It should be observed that in that country the word "city" is unknown; so that if they wished to speak of Paris, they would describe it by the phrase "the great village."

The position of this post is most advantageous, because it is on Lake Huron, through which all the tribes from the south are obliged to pass when they go down to Montreal and in coming back, as well as the French who wish to trade in the upper country. None of

ture of the life that centered there, see M. M. Quaife, *Lake Michigan* (Indianapolis, 1944), Chap. V. It immediately became the most important post in the western country, and the commandant had general oversight of all the western posts. The commandant from 1694 to 1697 was Antoine Lamothe Cadillac, author of the present memoir. The evacuation decree of 1696 compelled the return of the garrison to Lower Canada in 1697, following which Cadillac went on to Paris to lobby for the royal support of his project (effected in 1701) to establish a fort and colony on the strait connecting Lake Huron with Lake Erie. To his new post of Fort Pontchartrain du Detroit he attracted the Ottawa and others from the vicinity of Mackinac. In 1706, therefore, the Jesuits abandoned and burned the mission, which Marquette had founded in 1671. The modern city of St. Ignace was founded in the first half of the nineteenth century.

them can pass without being observed, for the horizon is so clear that canoes can be seen from the fort as far as the keenest sight can reach. In short, it may be said that this place is the center of the whole of this farther colony, where one is in the midst of all the other posts and almost at an equal distance from them, and among all the tribes which have dealings with us.

I do not know why the name "lakes" has been given to these watery deeps of such vast extent. However, the first is called Lake Superior, the second Lake Huron, the third Lake Michigan or Illinois, the fourth Lake Erie, and the fifth Lake Ontario. I think it important, and even necessary for the satisfaction of inquiring minds, to explain what reasons there may have been for dividing this single lake into five parts; I call it one only, because it is indisputable that it is one and the same body of water, communicating with and flowing from one to the other.

It is true there is a rapid at the village of the Sault de Sainte-Marie, so that any navigation in ships is impracticable there in either direction. It is therefore necessary to make a portage, that is to carry the baggage by land around the rapids. You can, however, run them in a canoe or a long-boat. This is the chief reason why Lake Superior, which is 500 leagues in circumference, has been divided from Lake Huron, which is 600 leagues round.

Now the latter is not separated from Lake Michigan; but it is maintained that they are not the same on account of a strait, two leagues wide, through which ships can pass quite safely. Once this strait is passed, Lake Michigan suddenly broadens and is about 300 leagues round.

Lake Erie is also separated from Lake Huron by a strait, through which ships can easily pass. It is 200 leagues round. This latter lake is separated from the first, Lake Ontario, also 200 leagues round, by an impassable waterfall which no ship can surmount.[2] Thus it will be easily understood that you can readily sail round these lakes for a distance of 1800 leagues, in fresh water and with land all around you, not only with canoes but even with barques and large vessels, except that ships on Lakes Huron, Michigan, and Erie cannot pass into Lake Superior nor Lake Ontario, where it would be necessary to build other barques or ships.

No bottom can be found well out into these lakes, any more than on the high seas; near the land, there is 20, 25, 30, 40 or 50 fathoms

[2] The Niagara.

of water almost everywhere. The current, especially near Michilimackinac is as rapid as on the ocean itself. Perhaps this might be attributed to the winds which are frequent there. But experience shows this is not so, for the currents are always contrary to the wind, without exception; so that, for example, if it is blowing from the north the current runs towards the north, and if it blows from the south the current runs towards the south, and so with the other winds; and, what is still more peculiar, during a calm the currents foretell the direction from which the wind is about to blow. This observation is unfailing. I leave it to the philosophers to reason upon the matter, assuring them that my testimony is as true as it is to say that there is daylight at high noon.

In Lake Michigan there is a tide, that is its waters ebb and flow every twenty-four hours, just as in the ocean, and the waves increase and diminish according to the course of the moon.[3]

There is a small lake ten leagues up country from Lake Michigan, remarkable for its

[3] The subject of tides on Lake Michigan has intrigued observers from the early French explorers down. Careful observations recorded in more recent decades disclose that there is indeed a tide, but so infinitesimal that it has no appreciable bearing on the lake levels.

perpetual movement. It is about two leagues long, and at each end there are a number of channels, dividing at various points, which might be taken for trenches made by man.

Now it happens that you sometimes see one end of this little lake dry and sometimes the other, and the streams or trenches adjacent to one another are now empty and now full to overflowing, so that its waters are continually agitated, rushing from one end to the other and chasing one another as if playing tag, and you would say it was some demon which was tossing them about in such a way.

Since I have shown the position of the fort and of the villages of the French and the Indians, I will now describe the manner in which the latter are built and fortified. Their forts are made of piles. Those in the outer row are as thick as a man's thigh and about 30 feet high; the second row, inside, is a full foot from the first, which is bent over on to it, and is to support it and prop it up; the third row is four feet from the second one, and consists of piles three and a half feet in diameter standing 15 or 16 feet out of the ground. Now, in this row they leave no space between the piles; on the contrary, they set them as close together as they can, making loop-holes at intervals. In the first two rows there is a space of about six inches between the piles, and thus the first and second rows do not prevent them from seeing the enemy; but there are neither curtains nor bastions and strictly speaking the fort is only an inclosure.

Their cabins are built like arbors. They drive poles into the ground as thick as one's leg and very long, and join them to one another by making them bend over at the top, and then tying and fastening them together with bass wood bark, which they use in the same way we use thread and rope. They then entwine between these large poles crosspieces as thick as one's arm, and cover them from top to bottom with the bark of fir-trees or cedars, which they fasten to the poles and the cross-branches; they leave an opening about two feet wide at the peak, which runs from one end to the other. Their cabins are weatherproof, and no rain gets into them; they are generally 100 to 130 feet long by 24 feet wide and 20 high. There is an elevated platform on each side, and each family has its little apartment. There is also a door at each end. Their streets are regular, like our villages.

The houses of the French are built of wood, one log upon another, but they are roofed with cedar bark.[4] Only the houses of the Jesuits are roofed with planks.

It should be borne in mind that four different tribes are included under the name Ottawa. The first is the Kiskakon, that is, the "Cut Tails," and it is the most numerous; the second is the Sable tribe, so called because their former dwelling place was in a sandy country, their village being in a sandy cove, but the Iroquois drove this tribe from its lands; the third is the Sinago, and the fourth the Nassauakuetoun, that is the Tribe of the Fork, a name derived from that of the Chief, or, much more probably, from the river from which they originally came, which divides into three branches, forming a sort of fork. These four tribes are allies and are closely united, living on good terms with one another, and now speak the same common language.

[4] This statement supplies one interesting refutation of the idea, fast becoming popular since the publication of Harold R. Shurtleff's *The Log Cabin Myth* in 1939, that log houses were unknown in interior America until their use by the Swedes of Delaware was adopted by other American colonists. It can hardly be maintained that the French architecture of seventeenth century Mackinac was influenced by the example of Swedish Delaware. Log houses were also built by the French at Detroit before the example of English settlers could have had any bearing upon the methods employed by their builders.

The Huron tribe is not incorporated with the other four. Moreover, its village is separated from theirs by a palisade. They speak a different language, so that the two only understand one another through interpreters. It was formerly the most powerful and also the most numerous tribe, but the Iroquois destroyed them and drove them from their homeland, so that they are now reduced to a very small number; and it is well for us that it is so. For they are cunning men, intriguing, evil-disposed and capable of great undertakings, but, fortunately, their arm is not long enough to execute them; nevertheless, since they cannot act like lions they act like foxes and use every possible means to stir up strife between us and our allies.[5]

As early as 1756, according to the captivity narrative of Charles Stuart, there were about 70 houses "built of Loggs & Covered with Boards of about one inch Thick Cut at a Saw Mill." Printed in *Miss. Valley Hist. Rev.*, XIII, 77.

[5] Despite this estimate of their character, following the founding of Detroit Cadillac invited the Huron to remove to that place. They did so, and continued their trouble-making propensities. About 1729 they removed their village to the site of present-day Amherstburg at the mouth of the Detroit. In 1748 they plotted the destruction of Detroit and the overthrow of their French "Father," a precursor of the design of Pontiac in 1763. The plot was scotched, however, and they were required to come back to the near vicinity of Detroit, where the

With regard to the land, each tribe has its own district and each family marks out its piece of land and its fields; the women look after the cultivation of the land and sowing it, and it is a real pleasure to see them, with a tool made of hard wood shaped like a hoe at one end and flat at the other, tilling the soil with incredible energy and industry. Their harvest consists of Indian corn, peas, beans, pumpkins, and water melons.

The great abundance of fish and the ease of catching them have caused the Indians to make a settlement in this region. It is a daily manna which never fails; there is no family which does not catch sufficient fish to live on throughout the year. Moreover, better fish can not be eaten, for it is bathed and nourished in the purest water, the clearest and most pellucid you could see anywhere.

I think it would be useless to explain the way in which they fish, since each tribe has

commandant could keep closer watch upon them. The site selected was Sandwich (now incorporated with Windsor); here, around the Huron mission, the second-oldest settlement in the Detroit River area grew up. The southerly exit from the Ambassador Bridge is today called Huron Line Road. The Huron were active in the Revolutionary warfare, being largely responsible for the overthrow of Colonel Crawford's army and for the slaughter of the pride of Kentucky's manhood at the Blue Licks.

its own method.[6] But I think I ought to mention the pleasure of seeing them bring up, in one net, as many as a hundred white fish. This is the most delicate fish in the lake. They are as large as shad in France. They also catch a large number of trout, weighing up to 50 pounds; they are certainly very good eating. Finally, the sturgeon, pike, carp, herring, dory, and a hundred different kinds of fish abound at this part of the lake.

It may be of interest also to state on what food the French and the Indians live, and how it is prepared. This is what they do:

They saw a big tree and cut a log about three feet long which they hollow out for about two feet, almost like a mortar. Then they make a pestle of hard wood, about five feet long; after this they put Indian corn into the mortar and crush it with the pestle. When it is sufficiently pounded they winnow it and the bran is separated, so that only the meal is left, which is sifted in order to remove the dust; the result is that the meal remains pure, clean, and white like rice. It is put into a cookingpot with water to boil; and at the same time they cook some white fish in an-

[6] For a more detailed description of the fish, and the methods of fishing, at Mackinac and the Sault see Alexander Henry's *Travels and Adventures*, the Lakeside Classics volume for 1921, pp. 55-57 and 61-62.

other pot; when they see that the meal is half cooked they take out the fish and soak it in the boiled meal, which is reduced to a white liquid like milk. They then throw it into the pot and stir it with a wooden spoon in the same way as one does rice, until it is thoroughly cooked; and as it is the custom of the country for each person to have his dish, each fills his own dish with this broth, which the Indians call *Sagamity*, that is to say, different things mixed together to be eaten.

This is not dainty food, but it is certainly very wholesome, for it always keeps the bowels open, and it is very aperitive, for one urinates as often as fifty times a day and if one never ate any other food he would never be thirsty, as many persons have found out who have gone whole months without thinking of drinking. I can affirm that I have gone twenty days without feeling the slightest thirst; which makes me think it would be a good diet for those who suffer from gravel. In the evening they eat fish cooked in all sorts of ways—fried, roasted, boiled, smoked, or stewed; they have neither oil nor butter, but they have grease or marrow from the elk, moose, or buffalo which is brought to Michilimackinac from the Illinois or from Chicago, and I really think that this flavoring is as good as that of the Carthusians or the Minims.

They make bread with the meal of Indian corn, which they bake under the ashes or in hot sand. It is good when one is hungry, and it is wonderfully fattening.

It is always healthy at Michilimackinac; this may be attributed to the good air or to the good food, but it is better to attribute it to both. A certain proof of the excellence of the climate is to see the old men there, whose grandsons are growing gray; and it would seem as if death had no power to carry off these specters. They have good hearing and good sight, but their memory often plays them tricks, for they sometimes claim that they are 150 or 200 years old. They tell tales and recount events which they maintain happened at that time, which is not credible; but they have this advantage, that there is no one who can contradict them or call them liars except by inference.

Beavers are very scarce in the neighborhood of Michilimackinac, and the Indians at this post go as far as 200 leagues to hunt for them. A good hunter does not generally kill more than fifty or sixty between October and May, sometimes more and sometimes less. They barter their beaver skins for our goods; this is what is called trading, or doing trade. We supply them with powder, bullets, arms, cloth, tobacco, and everything else we use.

If people could realize the labor which is involved in finding beaver skins they would not think so lightly of this commodity; for it should be known that the French trading-party generally leaves Montreal at the beginning of spring, or about the 15th of September, and in this country both seasons are bad—the first, because it is the time when the ice and snow melt, making the current strong and the water very cold, and the second because it is the beginning of the ice and snow. There are many rapids on the way. The Canadians, who are almost always indomitable fishermen, are generally bare-footed and bare-legged, wearing only their shirts; when their canoes cannot make headway against the rapids, they boldly jump into the water and by main strength, all helping one another, they manage to get them along, but not without frequently skinning their feet and legs for the rocks are so cold that their skin sticks to them and the men do not get free without leaving a piece behind them. If this happened only once a day it would be a small matter; but, on the contrary, it happens constantly throughout their entire voyage.

Nor is this all. They frequently come to rapids or waterfalls where it is impossible to take their boats up or down, and it is necessary to disembark at the foot of the rapids and carry the canoes on the men's shoulders through the woods, along with all the merchandise or beaverskins, around the falls before they can re-embark; this is called making a portage. Some of the portages are 200 leagues long.[7]

Thus the Canadians have to make a journey of 300 leagues by this continual and laborious work before reaching Michilimackinac, which shows their strength and vigor and how inured they are to fatigue; it seems incredible that the human body is able to withstand such extraordinary cold.[8]

When they arrive there, instead of trying to recover a little from their fatigue they hasten to continue their journey, and go on as soon as possible. They generally re-equip themselves here with canoes and provisions, after which some go to the north coast of Lake Superior and others to the south, and they follow the rivers into the back country for a distance of 200 or 300 leagues. Some of them, following Lake Michigan, go south to

[7] Probably a copyist's error for "two leagues."

[8] For a detailed narrative of the journey from Montreal to Mackinac as conducted by the traders of a subsequent generation see Alexander Henry, *Travels and Adventures*, Chaps. 2 and 3.

the most distant tribes. The object of all alike is to get beaver-skins.[9]

When the voyageurs have sold their goods they return to Michilimackinac, generally arriving at the beginning of July; here they re-equip themselves anew and go down to Montreal in a convoy, if the commandant of the country thinks it safe. It is plain, therefore, that those who engage in this trade for beaver skins have to travel at least 1000 leagues before getting back to Montreal; but aside from this it is difficult to conceive the dangers to which they are exposed in shooting whirlpools, falls, and rapids, which only to think of makes one's hair stand on end.

Nor is this all. They must also risk losing their lives by the hands of the Iroquois, who prepare ambushes in narrow passes along the route and if a man is captured alive he must be prepared to be burned to death by inches. It is true that all necessary precautions are taken to avoid this misfortune, and that it rarely happens that our convoys are defeated.

[9] A century and a quarter later the fur trade was being conducted in almost the identical fashion here described. Compare Gurdon L. Hubbard's description, as given in his *Autobiography*, the Lakeside Classics volume for 1911.

Chapter 2

DESCRIPTION OF THE INDIANS

ALL the Indians, generally speaking, are well-built, of fine stature, extremely wiry, vigorous, and strong, and of great endurance. They all have black eyes, large pupils, and good sight, keen and piercing; their hair is thick and black; their teeth are very white, small and regular. They have long necks, flat stomachs, large feet, and long legs; they have no hair on the face nor on any part of the body; and you rarely see anyone lame or hump-backed among them.

We may say without flattery that all the Indians are naturally intelligent; but, as their intellect is not cultivated, and they act only on their own inclinations in everything, their knowledge is restricted to what takes place in their own village or among their nearest neighbors; so that they look upon what Europeans tell them as so many fancies which their imagination delights to feed upon. It is easy to see that they have a charming imagination and very great facility for drawing, painting, and sculpture; and as they have no knowledge of letters or writing, God has given them, in place of this, a very good memory.

They have two tests of true men; the first is war and the second hunting. The best warriors and the best hunters are the men most valued, most important, and most praiseworthy among them; so that he who possesses these two qualities seems to be proclaimed as a chief among his tribe.

The fact that the hunter is accounted the equal of the warrior need cause no surprise; for it should be remembered that all the Indians live and maintain their families by their guns or, more properly speaking, by their cleverness, cunning, and skill in catching animals in the snares they lay for them. To succeed in this they must be familiar with the hunting grounds and know the trails, the haunts, and the instinct of wild animals; they must be able to bear fatigue and to be patient, lucky, eager, energetic, bold, and good runners; they must have a keen eye and sound wind. They hunt the elk, moose, hind, bear, roebuck, caribou, beaver, and buffalo. They have to kill these animals in the woods or on the prairies, by surprise or by swiftness of foot.

Whatever anyone may think, I know that you must have a good pair of legs to play this game. Yet a good hunter sometimes kills a dozen animals in a day, and it is a pleasure to see the Miami, from time to time, bringing into their village huge bears which they have captured and tamed, driving them before them with switches, like sheep driven to the shambles. It is on such occasions that good hunters show their prowess; and as it is true in every country that those who are fond of hunting pursue it for their own pleasure and satisfaction rather than for profit, money, or gluttony, so, among the Indians, the good hunters profit the least from their hunting. They often make feasts for their friends or relatives, or distribute the animals they have killed among the cabins or the families of the village. One proof of the liberality or the vanity which they acquire from this occupation is that those who are present when they arrive at their village are permitted to appropriate all the meat in the canoe of the hunter who has killed it, and he merely laughs. This is sufficient reason for believing that their only idea is to feed the people; and as the whole tribe gets the benefit, it is interested in praising such a noble calling, especially as it often happens that a single hunter provides food for several families which, but for his aid, would at certain times and places perish of hunger and want. It must not be thought altogether strange, therefore, that they think as highly of a hunter as of a warrior. The only difference I have found is that the one is more feared and distrusted, while the other is more loved and cherished.

In the matter of war all the Indians have the same strategy and the same custom and manner of fighting. Their war parties or companies are formed in this manner. A war chief abstains from eating and drinking, fasting sometimes for a week; he daubs and paints his whole face black; he says little, and ponders and dreams night and day, praying to the spirit he has chosen as his guardian or patron to give him men. This spirit, in whom he has confidence, is a crow, an eagle, an otter, a bear, a fox, or some other animal; but each looks up to his own, which is always the one which has appeared to him in his dreams and visions; so that, if during their sleep they see visions of their enemies at certain times and places, and if the vision has appeared favorable during their fast, they take it as a good omen and conclude that they will be victorious over their enemies.

As soon as this period of dreaming is over they wash their faces and paint them red, black, and white, but generally red only. They crop their hair and oil it, and clean up generally. Then they give a feast to the young men and to a few of the old ones, but

before they begin to eat the chief harangues
them in about these terms: "My brothers, it
is true that I am not a man; yet you know
that I have already faced the foe. Our men
have been killed. For a long time the bones
of so-and-so, our brother, have rested in such-
and-such a place. It is time for us to go and
see them. Now you know that he was a brave
man who deserves to be avenged. We have
rested in peace on our mat. Today I arise,
for the spirit who rules me has promised me
broth and fresh meat. Take courage, young
men, crop your hair, put on your war-paint,
fill your quivers, and let us console our dead;
let our war songs ring through the village,
awakening our brother who was slain; he will
be content when he has been avenged."

It should be observed that the Indians always call one another brothers or companions,
and that in this harangue the terms "broth"
and "fresh meat" mean killing men and capturing prisoners; "cropping the hair" means
taking off the garb of mourning; to put on
war-paint is to dress themselves up and
adorn themselves; to "rest on the mat" is to
repose and live in peace. They never speak
of those whom they have killed, but only of
their own dead.

When the chief has finished his speech
they answer him by a loud confused cry, to

show that they applaud him and approve his
plan. After this, the chief, or another person
nominated by him, rises from his seat with a
quiver in his hand and sings a war-song.
Usually this is merely a repetition of what
was said in the harangue. They chant thus,
one after another, especially those who wish
to take part in the expedition. Then they eat
what has been prepared; only the man who
is giving the feast will eat nothing, content-
ing himself with smoking a few pipes of tobacco. As soon as the meal is finished they
beat the drum constantly until the war party
is complete.

On the day of departure the warriors deck
themselves out as finely as possible. They
redden their hair; they paint their faces red
and black, very artistically and prettily, as
well as their entire body. Some wear head-
dresses made of the tails of eagles or other
birds; others adorn themselves with the
teeth of fierce wild animals, such as wolves
and tigers; some, instead of a hat, fit their
head-dress with the horns of a stag, roebuck,
or ox. They gird themselves with their bows,
quivers, and arrows. Their canoes are painted
various colors and are ornamented on the
prow with figures or with the arms of the
leader; you see on them the war-mat, the
crow, the bear, or some other animal such as

I have already mentioned—the guardian spirit which is to guide the enterprise.

As soon as they embark they push their canoes fifteen or twenty yards out and range them in line, close together, the end of one not projecting beyond the other, in which they are very particular. The chief of the party then stands up in the middle of his canoe, holding in his hand a gourd with little stones inside it. He shakes it, chanting an invocation to his guardian spirit, to give him a prosperous journey. The warriors respond to his chant with a double guttural *"Che,"* while the other chiefs, on shore, harangue at the same time, exhorting the young men to fight well, to watch the route both in front and behind them on their journey, to scout well, and not to allow themselves to be taken by surprise.

The war-chief, who all this time has been singing in his canoe, begs all the village not to forget them if they are killed, but to remember to avenge them. This done, they give a great shout all together and start off at the same moment in the direction they are to go, as if they saw the enemy before them, their canoes speeding onward like arrows. These trappings of war are dreadful indeed to those who have never seen them before or who are not accustomed to them.

When they reach the enemy's country they proceed warily; they keep silence, observe everything, and never fire their guns. If they come upon the trail of any one they can easily distinguish whether it is old or recent; they know the number of people who have passed there, and how many days ago their journey was made; and as they know when their enemies went by, they can tell pretty nearly where they will be, and from this they determine whether to pursue them or to go in search of others.

One might say that these people are guided by instinct rather than by knowledge or reason, for if one man or a number are discovered their doom is almost always certain and unfailing. It is in vain that they try to escape by walking on moss or leaves, or through marshes, or even over rocks; every precaution they may take to conceal their tracks is quite useless, for their pursuers are rarely mistaken. The strangest thing is that they know by the impress of the foot, or its shape, to what tribe the people in front of them belong.

When they conclude that they are fairly near their enemies they despatch their best runners to go and spy out their camp, where they are to pass the night, and to see what weapons they have, and how the place lies.

These scouts must possess cunning, experience, and boldness; for it should be understood that all war parties on the march send out scouts for three or four leagues round the spot where they wish to encamp or sleep, and when the scouts return to their encampment without seeing anything, and make their report, all the others, relying on them, sleep peacefully all night, it being their custom not to post any guard or sentry.

On the other hand, those who have discovered the enemy, after observing them carefully, return to the main body or the appointed place of meeting, and on their report a council is held. Then, if they think they are strong enough to attack, they go at once, generally by night, with the scouts at their head, who never lose their impression of the road nor of the encampment of their enemies. When they are near enough they throw themselves flat on the ground, with eyes and ears alert and the scouts in front and rear and on both flanks. In this posture they wait until daybreak, as that is the time when a man is heaviest from the desire for sleep, and also that they may be able to see better when they make their onslaught and to take advantage of the remainder of the day for making their retreat. Their custom is to drag themselves along the ground on all fours like cats, and approach within pistol shot; they then stand up before shooting. The leader gives his signal by a low cry. The others immediately give a loud whoop, and if they have guns they fire all together at the enemy; if not, they let fly their arrows. After their first volley, if they see that the enemy is thrown into disorder and routed, they rush upon them, hatchet or tomahawk in hand; if they are victorious they take the scalps of those who are killed.

If they capture any prisoners they pinion them so tightly that the bonds cut into their flesh. Then they travel night and day until they are out of danger and safe from their enemies. When they are near their own village they send men ahead to give the news of all that has happened during the campaign, after which preparations are made for welcoming the warriors and haranguing them before they enter the place. At the same time arrangements are made for the entrance of the prisoners, which always begins with from three to four hundred blows with sticks, making them fall flat on their faces a hundred times before they enter the cabin of triumph which has been prepared for them.

As soon as they are within, they are told to dance and chant their death song. The chant is both proud and mournful; they recite what they have done during their lives, especially

the number of persons they have killed, with
their names and the names of their tribes, the
place and how they did the deed. Sometimes
they are made to sit and sometimes to get up,
and always to chant, especially when anyone
of importance comes into the cabin to see
them. But while they are singing in this way
one man pulls out a finger-nail, another puts
one of their fingers in the pipe he is smoking;
at intervals a firebrand is held to their flesh,
which is burned down to the bone; some cut
off pieces of their flesh, which they cook and
eat immediately, sucking their fingers afterward as if they had eaten something exqui-
site. Thus they amuse themselves for two or
three days, after which the old men, the war
chiefs, and the principal men of the village
assemble to determine the life or death of
these unfortunates.

Their death or life generally depends upon
the women, for this reason. Some of them
have lost a husband or sons in the war, and
if seeing a handsome prisoner, or more often
actuated merely by whim or caprice they ask
for them to replace the dead, the council
never refuses them. As soon as they are de-
clared free they are unbound and the women
or girls who have saved them lead them to
their cabins. They wash their wounds, oil
them, and make them look as well as they

can; and a few days later a feast is given in the cabin at which the strangers are adopted as children of the house, as brothers, sons-in-law, or other relatives.

From this time they are treated kindly and no one insults them any more. But the most surprising thing is that they are the first to go to war against their own tribe, and kill or take prisoners their fathers, uncles, or other relatives indifferently, as if they were nothing at all to them, thinking more of the second life which has been given them than of the life they received from their fathers and mothers, whom they often see burned and torn in pieces because they were hard-hearted enough not to set them at liberty after capturing them; for, as I have already said, the life or death of the slaves depends either on the council or the women. The council gives some of them to the French commandant and others to various tribes, to confirm and ratify their alliances. As soon as they have handed them over they cease to have control of them, and their life or death depends on their new masters or the tribe to which they are presented.

The common custom is to put them to death, in the manner we shall presently describe; but as we have seen that the council of the old men grants slaves their lives at the request of the women, so, also, if the latter wish them to die this request is never refused; and since human nature, especially in the female sex, is better pleased by vengeance than by pardon, the fate of the slaves is almost always unhappy. If one of them is sometimes spared, it is apparently only by a miracle of predestination. The great majority of the women love to avenge the relatives whom they have lost, which they pretend to do by putting to death those whom the fortune of war has placed in their power. Finally, when these poor wretches, whether Frenchmen or savages, are condemned to death, this is the strange and terrible manner in which it is done.

These furies, filled with bitter memories and resentment for the death of their relatives, who have already met a similar fate, seize upon the victims. First they caress them and take them to their cabins. They anoint them and give them food, urging them to fill their stomachs well, for they say that as they have a long journey to make they should eat a good meal, or conserve strength to suffer the longer and more courageously. To see them doing these things, you would think that they were acting out of friendship or pity; but the victims, who know that it is otherwise, do not delight in attentions of this sort, for they know that the food they eat will be hard to digest. While they are receiving all these kind attentions from the women, the young men are planting stakes to which these unfortunates are to be tied and are preparing the fires, the tools, the irons, and all the instruments they can invent to satisfy and glut their rage and fury.

When all these preparations are finished, they send word to the women who are fondling the poor victims. Suddenly their feminine sweetness changes into despair and diabolical fury; and this is the way the woman who has demanded a prisoner's death informs him of the fate which awaits him. She calls upon the shade of her husband or son, or whatever relative has been killed or burned, and speaks in these terms:

"Come hither, my son, and take courage; today I have a feast of fresh meat for you. Drink of this broth; accept the sacrifice I am making of this brave warrior. Rejoice, my dear son, he will be roasted and burned, all his nails will be torn off, this meat will be roasted, and some of it will be cooked in the pot, he will have necklaces of hatchets redhot from the fire hung round him, his fingers will be calmly smoked; his genitals will be torn out; we will drink from his skull, we will tear off his scalp. Be content, my son, and rest now, for you will be avenged."

One of the warriors now enters the cabin and says to the man who has already been told of his doom, "Take courage, my brother, you are to be burned." The other replies "All right, and thanks for the news you bring me." At the same moment a horrible cry is raised throughout the village. This cry is called a *Sakakua*. They seize him, take him away and fasten him to the stake by the feet, the hands, and the middle of the body; there he is to play the most tragic role that one can possibly conceive, for the old woman who sacrifices him predicts but a portion of the pain and torment which her victim is about to undergo in memory of the one to whom he is sacrificed. These sinister preparations, which should make the man for whom they are intended shudder (I speak of the Indians) only serve him, however, as a means of showing his scorn for his tyrants. He is no sooner bound to the stake than he chants his death song in a firm and bold voice, recounting all the warlike deeds he has done during his life and the manner in which he has burned his prisoners, encouraging those around him not to spare him, and to put him to death like a warrior. I do not think that all this talk is entirely sincere; it is certain, however, that his mind does not appear to be disturbed, as shown by the fact that his gaze is steadfast and his countenance tranquil.

But it is time to open the ball and see how the chief actors are made to dance. The first step the prisoners are put through is tearing the nails from their hands, one after another, with the teeth. The pipes and calumets of the Indians are made of a sort of stone which is easily hollowed out and is not brittle. They fill them with tobacco and put the victim's fingers in the bowl of the pipe and thus smoke the ten fingers, one after another. After this little feast, five or six workers take up burning fire-brands; they apply them to his ankles, wrists, and temples, and do not take them away until nerves and flesh are burned to the bone. This is the second step of the minuet. The third is a necklace of glowing hatchets, made red hot in the fire, which falls over the shoulders and on to the stomach of the captive, and are not removed until they are cold; and since those who do this work have good appetites, each of them cuts off a piece of the buttocks with his knife, which he broils and eats at once without any seasoning; and to wash the wounds and the blood which flows from them, the women have kettles of boiling water ready, which they pour over them. From time to time they pierce his neck and armpits with red-hot irons. They burn his genitals with birch-bark, which gives a very hot and penetrating flame; and to make an end of these horrible details, it is sufficient to say that they do not leave him a nerve or an artery which has not been subjected to the fire or the knife.

Last of all they take off his scalp and this is done with such art and skill that they get it off all in one piece, like a wig. Having done this, they throw handfuls of hot ashes and sand upon the raw and bleeding flesh, and when they see that it is mummified they give him the *coup de grace* with a blow of a hatchet on his head, or stab him two or three times in the heart. They cut off his head, while all the village resounds with shouts of joy and delight, as if they had won some great victory. Whoever reads this short description may perhaps have difficulty in believing it, and in persuading themselves that any one can bear such suffering and burning without dying; but it is absolutely true, and this terrible practice is especially common with the Iroquois, who burn their slaves by inches for five or six days on end.

It might also be thought that anyone tortured in this way must sometimes shed tears or, in the extremity of his torment, utter pitiful cries. There are indeed some who cannot refrain from doing so, but most of them seem to ignore their pain and pretend to know nothing of what is happening to them; for instead of asking mercy they taunt their tormenters, calling them cowards and women who lack the courage to cut them up into bits; and if any part of them has escaped being burned, they point it out themselves and beg them not to spare them, bearing all these barbarities from beginning to end without even a wry face. They only ask for a smoke or for a drink of water, which is never refused, their object being to gain new strength in order to enable their enemies to exercise their ferocious cruelty upon them longer; and they speak to them like this: "Take courage, my brothers, amuse yourselves today; and if you are ever taken prisoner by my tribe and are burned in my village, do not weep or cry out, but smoke quietly like me. It is only women who are permitted to shed tears; a true warrior should die as I do."

Their vanity and their desire to be considered brave is the sole source and motive of the indifference they show to suffering and torture; and the form and manner of this punishment are simply a method of intimidating and giving pause to those who follow the occupation of war. This practice of torture was formerly held in horror by the

French; but when it was perceived that humanity shown for these savages was regarded by them as cowardice, and induced them to attack the French more frequently because, at the worst, they only risked being captured or killed, the French finally adopted the practice of burning them with all sorts of cruelty—so true it is that if you consort with wolves you must howl as they do.

This course was adopted only too late. It is now evident that their raids are less frequent and their attacks less bold. In a word, they value their lives as much as others do; and although they are brave enough to show such great fortitude and scorn of death when they are in the hands of their enemies, it is no less true that they take not only every possible precaution to avoid being captured in combat, but also that the idea of being taken alive to be afterwards exposed to the extremity of torture is terrible and frightful to them. This explains why they always make surprise attacks, and those who are surprised are always beaten. However, in such a strait they take to their heels, and some of them often escape; but if they find themselves so hard pressed that it is impossible to escape and they are compelled to fight against a superior force, they fight desperately and sell their lives dearly. Such is the practice of nearly all these tribes with regard to war and hunting.

Chapter 3

WE shall now consider various other customs common to them, such as marrying or living with as many women as they please, provided they can support them. When they are tired of them or find them troublesome, they cast off such of them as they think fit and replace them by others if the fancy takes them; and in the same way, if the women are not satisfied with their husbands they abandon them and go and live with another more to their liking. By this means nothing is ever lost, for one takes what the other gives up; and by these very natural and convenient customs they get rid of all the rancor and hatred that troubles family life. Nevertheless it rarely happens that a husband dismisses his wife, or a wife leaves her husband, if they have children. But if it does happen, all the offspring, both boys and girls, belong to the mother, and the husband is not allowed to retain any of them against her will; for the mother's title rests on the law of nature, since no one can dispute that she is the mother of the children whom she has brought into the world, while the identity of the father is always uncertain, and often unknown.

For this reason the Indians trace their genealogy through the women, when they wish to prove their claim to nobility. Among them the number of children is never a burden to the mother. On the contrary, she is more highly respected for them, more honored, more esteemed, and richer. Accordingly she finds it an easier and quicker matter to get married again, for the man who marries her, in becoming her husband becomes also the father and head of the whole family, and is therefore a person of more importance; for if the children are grown-up they support the cabin either by their deeds as warriors or by hunting, or by the alliances they make by taking wives of their own; and if they are still young, the step-father hopes and expects that if he receives any personal wrong or injury he will be avenged when his stepsons, who regard him as their own father, are old enough. Moreover this actually happens, for the Indians love nothing so much as revenge, and this is why widows who have children easily find a husband.

But if a man becomes a widower and his wife leaves him children, then the relatives pick out a wife for him suitable to his circumstances. They make the proposal to her and take her to his cabin. If he refuses her, and in course of time takes another more to his liking, the woman who has received this insult is allowed to abuse him and heap all sorts of insults upon him. Then she smashes up everything in the cabin or plunders and carries off all the finest and best things it contains and takes them to her own home, and neither the man nor his wife, who is considered as a concubine, can stop her or say a word to her, but only hang their heads. They seem to be covered with confusion, but really they are only laughing. After the woman has taken her revenge in this way she is satisfied, and says no more about the matter.

If a married man dies without issue and has one or more brothers living, one of them marries the widow, as if to raise up children to his dead brother, and it sometimes happens that they marry two sisters. They recognize no degree of relationship with regard to women as forming an obstacle to marriage. They use the same terms and descriptions of relationship as we do, such as grandfather, grandmother, son-in-law, uncle, nephew, and the rest.

Fathers and mothers love their children devotedly and permit them to make use of everything in the cabin and to consult on the affairs of the family. From this it arises that

sisters have more respect for their brothers than for their parents; so that when a
brother makes any reasonable request of his
sister, she never refuses what he asks. When
they are together, if anyone says anything
unseemly, blushes suffuse their faces and
they lower their eyes and are confused, which
proves the great respect they have for one
another.

When a woman is confined, she sleeps apart
and remains separated from her husband for
forty days; on the forty-first day she comes
into her cabin, where she makes a new fire
with a flint and steel, and then she is purified.
When the women or girls have their monthly
periods they leave their cabins and each one
lodges by herself. The others bring them
food in a dish, which they leave at their door,
but will not enter nor go near them. As soon
as they get over this indisposition they go
back to their cabins.

When the women are with child, or nursing, their husbands refrain from sleeping
with them, for they maintain that sexual
intercourse ruins the nourishment which the
child receives from its mother, weakens it,
and may cause an abortion. As for nursing
mothers, the Indians say that such intercourse spoils their milk and that if they become pregnant they could not nourish the

child, having no other food to give it. But the husbands are often duped, for their wives are not satisfied with such arguments and go and gratify themselves secretly elsewhere, paying but little attention to this regimen. However, it is true that there are many who do observe this custom, out of affection for their offspring.

This is the way they hold their feasts for the dead. They erect a cabin about 120 feet long, with new bark which has never been used before. They set up a maypole at each end and a taller one in the middle. These poles are oiled, greased, and painted, and at the top of each is placed a prize, which belongs to the person who can first reach it with his hand. Then they enter this new cabin, in which there are several platforms, bringing the bones of their relatives which are in small bags or wrapped very neatly in strips of bark. They arrange them from one end of the cabin to the other, and put with them all their finest and best possessions, generally including whatever they have accumulated in the last three years. Meanwhile, the kettles are constantly on the fire, full of meat, for anyone to eat who likes.

They make a continual racket night and day with drums or by striking the kettles or the strips of bark with sticks. From time to time they go out and surround the cabin, firing muskets and howling until the whole air trembles, after which they re-enter, bedaubed with black. This uproar goes on for three days and three nights; but before the time has quite expired they give to those who have been invited to the feast everything that belongs to the dead, all the booty with which the bones were covered. When this has been distributed they go out for the last time and surround the cabin, uttering great howls; they fall upon it with heavy blows of sticks and clubs, making a terrific uproar, and break all the bark in pieces.

This done, the women are ready with pine faggots, of which they make a layer on the ground from one end of the cabin site to the other. At the same time they kill a large number of dogs, which are to them what sheep are to us, and are esteemed by them more than any other animal, and make a feast of them. But before eating they set up two tall poles and fasten a dog to the top of each, which they sacrifice to the sun and the moon, praying to them to have pity and to take care of the souls of their relatives, to light them on their journeys, and to guide them to the dwelling-place of their ancestors. This idea proves that they believe in the immortality of the soul. The feast being thus concluded, they each take up the bones of their relatives and carry them to some stony place, hollow, rugged, and unfrequented. There they leave them, and that is the end of the ceremony. After this, the dead whose feast they have held are never spoken of again in any way, and they remain in perpetual oblivion.

They believe that the souls, when separated from the body, loiter and remain in the village, wandering to and fro in and around their cabins by a natural attachment, on account of their love for their relatives and friends. They also say that they frighten little children, young people, and themselves, especially at night. They imagine that the great racket and the hammering and breaking of the bark vexes the souls which have assembled in the cabin, inducing them to go and join the souls of their fathers. They believe that these are in a fine country, where life is most pleasant; and, because in their own land there are quantities of strawberries and raspberries, they imagine that in the country where the souls dwell these berries are as big as a man's head. They think this region is towards the east, that the air is mild and temperate, that there is neither rain nor snow nor wind, nor rocks nor mountains there, and that all the paths are paved with robes of otter, martens, and beaver; in a word, that it is a land of pleasure, where there is neither hunger nor thirst and where all are equally happy. They refuse to believe there are places where souls are tortured, and they reject the doctrine of the resurrection of the body.

Although among Europeans daughters are a burden and one is practically compelled to give them a dowry in order to marry them, among the Indians they are the wealth of their parents; for whoever wishes to marry a girl has to buy her with a large present, which he makes to his intended father-in-law or, if he is dead or absent, to her nearest relative. First, however, he must obtain the consent of his mistress, and there, as elsewhere, lovers go courting, talk amorous nonsense, and give one another tokens of respect and affection. The girls have this advantage, that they are allowed to enjoy themselves and try experiments with marriage as long as they like and with as many boys as they wish without reproach, nor does this prevent them from finding a husband when they are in the humor to do so.

This is the way they conduct their love-making. The young men have strips of bark rolled up in the form of a torch. At night they light one end and go through all the cabins they care to visit. The girls are lying down at the side of the passage-way, and when their beloved passes they stop him by seizing a corner of his garment. When the gallant perceives this signal he stoops down, and then his mistress takes his torch and puts it out and makes the young man lie down beside her, and he tells her his love. Despite this privacy and complete freedom, it is not often that anything takes place but what is quite seemly and respectful, so true it is that people think less of what is permitted than of what is forbidden. For it is evident that on these occasions there is nothing to prevent the lovers from indulging their passion; yet generally they do not, especially if they intend to marry. At length, when the girl is tired and wants to go to sleep she tells her lover, who retires as soon as she bids him. This custom is called by them "running the light." Married women, however, are obliged to proceed differently, for they are roughly chastised in some tribes, though not in all, if convicted of licentiousness, as I shall show elsewhere.

Every tribe has its doctors, surgeons, and apothecaries, who are called jugglers. When someone is sick they send for all three of them, and the doctor diagnoses the illness. After considering for a long while, they generally order several dogs to be killed, because this is their most delicious meat. To cloak the quackery they insist that two should be white, two black, and two of some other color, and they offer one or two of them as a sacrifice to the sun or the moon, praying them to take pity on the patient. This ceremony is only performed after long contemplation, for the jugglers or charlatans never attribute the cause of the sickness to the ailments or accidents which come upon the human body, but pretend that a spell has been cast on the patient by the malice or ill-will of some enemy. They make believe that a guardian spirit, that is, the imaginary god whom they have invented, has revealed to them how the poison and spell have been cast upon the sick man. The doctor therefore completes his performance by indicating to the apothecary the herbs and roots or animals necessary for compounding the antidotes or beverages to expel the poisons at work in the body and mind of the patient. The apothecary executes the doctor's order and seeks the simples or animals specified, but both of them play their parts very well, for these things, they say, are never found without great difficulty.

The surgeon is the greatest charlatan of all, and the most remarkable juggler. The part he plays is certainly humble to all appearance, and those who watch his performance can scarcely imagine that he is not possessed by a demon while he is doing his juggling. Those who stand around beat drums and strike the kettles and strips of bark with sticks, and this continues as long as the illness lasts, for the entertainment of the sick man. It is inconceivable why such an uproar does not drive the poor man crazy. While this is going on the surgeon dances, sings, makes frightful contortions, rolls his eyes, rubs his nose, gnashes his teeth, and sticks out his chin; his neck now stretches and now shortens; his lungs expand and his stomach swells; his fingers, hands, and arms are extended and withdrawn; he spits blood, and makes it issue from his nose and his ears, he tears his flesh, and, as I have already said, does these and many other things while continuing to chant and dance.

Finally, after all these proceedings, he discovers the spot where the man is bewitched; thus, if he sees that the sick man has difficulty in spitting or breathing, he makes him believe that the spell which has been cast upon him is a bone which has become caught in his throat. He approaches the patient with many grimaces; he seizes him by the throat with his teeth, but quite gently, pretending to look for the bone, which he always finds because he has one in his mouth. So, after making much fuss about the search, he jumps up suddenly, uttering a joyful cry to show that the spell is removed, and spits out the bone. Thereupon everyone present marvels at his art and cleverness, and the sick man begins to think he is healed.

In a word all his science consists in finding out the part which is affected, which is made known to him by the sufferer, upon which he says there is a bone or a gun screw, a thorn, a fish-bone, some hair, or something of the kind in the part affected. But if the sick man does not improve and his disease continues to grow worse, the surgeon continues to juggle, and keeps picking out some bewitched piece of something; while the apothecary, on his side, works with his medicines. When the patient dies they withdraw, like our physicians, saying that nothing could save him. Whichever way it turns out, these quacks ruin and impoverish the cabin or family of the sick person; for if he recovers he gives them everything he possesses, and the whole family does likewise, while if he dies they make him a large present notwithstanding.

These medicine men are respected and esteemed among all the tribes. They are clever enough to distinguish themselves from the rest by their manners and actions, which are

outwardly better regulated and more re-
strained; their gait is also slower and more
dignified than that of the others. When they
go anywhere, they wear round their necks or
on the shoulder or arm the skin of an otter or
some other animal, prettily decorated; and
it is by this sign that their doctors are recog-
nized, just as one recognizes monks by their
hoods. This shows that all over the world
some men gull others, and that, above all,
there are cheats and charlatans in the school
of Galen and Hippocrates.

Yet it is quite certain that all the Indians
are very clever and expert in healing all kinds
of sores and wounds, of whatever kind they
may be, by the use of herbs, of which they
have a thorough knowledge. They also have
remedies for burns, frost-bites, and the stings
and bites of snakes and other venomous animals; but the best of it is that they cure the
illness as quickly as it came. They are very
good anatomists and when an arm is frac-
tured or a bone broken they treat it with
great skill and dexterity, and experience
shows that they can cure a wounded man in
a week better than our surgeons can in a
month, either because they have better remedies or are more straight-forward, while our
doctors seek to turn their talent to their own
profit. They make light of venereal diseases,

for those who are attacked recover in ten or twelve days at the latest, by taking certain tasteless powders which they swallow in hot water, and for this reason one never sees any syphilitics among them, but they maliciously refuse to teach the French their secrets, though they do not refuse to treat them in case of need.

Chapter 4

ALL these tribes, without exception, have a tradition of the Flood; we shall see what their ideas are on this subject. They say that such a great quantity of snow and rain fell that all the waters, being gathered together, rose higher than the highest mountains, so that people went about everywhere in canoes and the earth was changed into a vast lake. But they maintain that in this universal flood, in which everyone perished, an old man in each tribe was saved, with all his family, because they had the sense when they saw the waters rising to build a very big canoe in which they put provisions and animals of all kinds, and after spending many days in great discomfort they threw an otter out of the boat to see whether he could not get to land somewhere; but they say the otter was drowned, for after some days he was seen floating on the water, on his back. After some time the old man sent a beaver in the opposite direction to see whether he could not find land. They say he found a sort of dam of dry wood, but because he was hungry he returned to the canoe, bringing back

a big stump, which made the old man conclude that the waters were beginning to fall;
then they turned their canoes toward the
spot from which they had seen the beaver
returning and at length they saw in the distance a great pile of wood, which had collected in the following manner:

They say that an enormous turtle fell from
the sky and floated under water; and as there
was a quantity of dry wood around, and other
trees with their roots and branches carried
hither and thither by the wind and the water,
those which came against the turtle fastened
to him and remained there, so that in a short
time such a large quantity accumulated that
one could walk on it as on a raft. When the
old man saw this, he landed on it, and finding
a little earth on the roots of the trees he collected it and offered it as a sacrifice to the sun,
which dried it. Then the old man, after re-
ducing it to dust, sowed it broadcast over the
waters, so that it drank up the water with
which the earth was covered. Each tribe
maintains that the turtle which fell from the
sky stopped on the highest mountain in their
part of the country, so that there is no agree-
ment where the place was.

If the statements set forth in this chapter
are considered attentively the reader may
think, as I do, that all these tribes are de-

scended from the Hebrews and were originally Jews, which may also be observed from the terms they use in conversation and in their speeches and customs.

The Jews formerly called one another brothers and companions; the Indians do the same. The Jews annointed and perfumed their hair; the Indians oil and grease theirs. The Jews fought desperately and in an undisciplined manner to preserve their liberty, preferring to kill their parents and their wives and children and themselves rather than to fall into the hands of their enemies alive. The Indians are so jealous of their liberty that they defend it to the death, and think there is nothing in the world so shameful to a man as slavery. For this reason they never leave anything in the hands of their prisoners which could aid in their destruction, for they kill themselves at the first opportunity: and when they are in the midst of torture, they display a degree of fortitude which amazes their tormentors. The Jews were uneasy, restless, seditious, jealous of the prosperity of their neighbors, even when they were of the same race as themselves and this is the real character of the Indians also.

The Jews were fond of war, assemblies, councils, and speeches, and under some fine pretext they were always indulging in acts of perfidy, treasons, and horrible massacres. The Indians cannot live without frequent feasting; councils and assemblies are their daily bread; and while they are pretending to be negotiating for friendships and alliances, whether with friends or enemies, they watch for an opportunity of making a good stroke as they call it, that is, of destroying them utterly in their characteristic fashion.

The Jews believed in dreams and visions, and the Indians believe that in their sleep a guardian spirit shows them their destiny, and especially what is to happen to them on their war forays.

The Jews married several wives, and put them away whenever they pleased; the Indians follow the same practice. When a Jew who was married died without issue, his widow went to his younger brother to learn whether he would marry her. If he refused her, she shook the dust from her shoes on the threshold of his door and spat in his face. If an Indian widower rejects the woman whom his relatives choose for him, she abuses him and breaks or carries off whatever she finds in his cabin. The younger brother among the Jews married the widow of his elder brother, if the latter died without issue. The Indian in like case marries his brother's widow. Jewish women, after giving birth to a child, were not purified and did not enter the temple until forty days had elapsed. As the savages have no house of prayer, the wives do not re-enter their cabins to sleep with their husbands until forty days after their delivery. Jewish women during their monthly periods, and men who lost their seed, did not enter the temple; Indian women while suffering from this indisposition leave their cabins and make one apart, and hold no communication either with men or with other women.

Jewish women, when with child, did not sleep with their husbands or have intercourse with them; Indians at such times have separate beds. The Jews paid the greatest honor to their dead and were most careful as to the right of burial; the Indians hold nothing so precious as the bones of their dead, and preserve them as relics. The Jews held feasts and made prayers to God, interceding for those who were dead; and the Indians hold feasts and festivals and make presents and sacrifices to the Sun and Moon for the souls of their relatives.

The Jews prayed to God to take the souls of their relatives to Eden, that is, to the garden or paradise of delight. The Indians pray to the Sun to guide and light the spirits of their tribe during their journey until they reach the happy dwelling-place of their ancestors.

The sect of the Essenes among the Jews believed that souls, on quitting their bodies, crossed the western sea and went to dwell in islands of delight, where sugar and all sorts of pleasant things abounded, where the air was soft and mild and exceedingly pure, and that they were exempt there from all the woes met with in the present life; and the Indians believe that their souls go to a region towards the east, where they have everything in abundance, where it is never cold nor hot, a country carpeted with the skins of martens and all kinds of furs.

The sect of the Sadduces among the Jews denied that souls were either tortured or honored, as well as denying the resurrection; and the Indians will not even listen to a word of the pains of hell, and say that such statements are lies invented to inspire fear, for they cannot understand that one who is dead can rise and live again. The Jews spoke in parables and metaphysically, and the Indians scarcely ever talk in any other way.

Finally, while it is from the Jews that we learn how the Deluge came, we see that the Indians also know about it. Nor is there any occasion for surprise at their fictions on this and so many other subjects; for if the Jews, who were so near to God and concerned for their history went astray, and if so many other peoples who have had the resource of writing to supply any defect of memory have plunged into an abyss of legends, how could the Indians, who know nothing of reading and writing, have retained what so many centuries have effaced? So I believe, from the observations I have just set forth that many people will be convinced that they are descended from the Jewish race, since their manners, customs, and ceremonies resemble those of the Jews more closely than any other nation. We shall see, also, in various passages of this Memoir, other details which will confirm the preceding ones and will complete, as far as possible, the proof of my theory; but to find out by what route the tribes have spread into the New World—that is the secret.[10]

It might be thought that if the Indians are really descended from the Jews they would at least have retained their language, since it is not natural that children should forget

[10] The theory of the Jewish origin of the Indians persisted until well into the nineteenth century. Present-day scholars commonly agree that the American continents were peopled at a much later date than the Euro-Asian, and theorize that the ancestors of the Indians migrated from Asia by way of Bering Strait and Alaska.

what their fathers and mothers have taught them from the time they began to lisp; and it is much more probable that habits, manners, and customs should pass away than the operations of the mind, which cannot be expressed nor known except by means of signs and words, which are lost only by the decay of the organs of the human body.

It seems to me that we may reply to this objection, that a language that is badly taught rusts and perishes completely, as everything else does in the course of time. Reason and experience teach us that a language becomes disfigured and weakened in proportion to its neglect and misuse. It is evident that Latin, so esteemed in the world, would have been lost and have disappeared if its purity had not been carefully preserved at all times by books and volumes which the ravages of time have spared so that we still have them. But if at the time of the Caesars all Latin documents had been destroyed, and afterwards no one had been able to write in that language, it is plain that its use would have become so corrupted and changed that if those who spoke it originally were to talk to men of the present age they would not understand one another at all.

Nor is it surprising that a people who have been wanderers and vagrants for so many centuries, and never accustomed to writing or reading—which are the foster-mothers of a language—should have so corrupted and debased it that scarcely any trace of it now remains. And there is no cause for surprise, that we find so many different languages among the Indians, for it is evident that Jerusalem was full of all sorts of tribes which had submitted to circumcision and were included in the Jewish nation, as we see in the speech made by Eleazar to the people; and the same may be observed in the Acts of the Apostles, chapter 2, which says that there were in that city men of every tribe under the sun, Parthians, Medes, Elamites, etc. It may be conjectured from this that the Jews, though they included all the circumcised foreigners as regards the observance of all the laws and customs, and all formed but one body, had nevertheless introduced a diversity of languages into their books which the inhabitants of the New World may have allowed to fall into disuse.

Chapter 5

AS I have described Michilimackinac in the first chapter, it would be useless to say any more about it. I will only mention that the word Ottawa means "Tribe with the Pierced Noses"; they pierce the nose and attach to it a small stone prettily ornamented, which comes down to the middle of the mouth, between the lips. It is a fashion with them, and they would not consider themselves in style if it were wanting. Some of the old men, however, maintain that it is a charm against medicine, that is, against the spells which their enemies or other malicious persons might cast upon them to poison them or compass their death.

This is further proof that it is an idea derived from the ancient Jews for we see from history that one Eleazar delivered men possessed of devils, in the presence of the Emperor Vespasian, his son, and several princes and lords of his Court. He proceeded thus. He pierced the nose of the man who was possessed, and passed a hollow ring through it,

in which he inclosed an herb; and as soon as
the demon smelt it he threw his subject to
the ground and took to flight, without daring
to re-enter him; and Eleazar often did this in
the name of Solomon. Thus these Indian
tribes may very likely have retained the custom of piercing their noses, and forgotten the
reason for which it was introduced.

There is a place near Michilimackinac
called Essolon. When I went there, my attention was drawn to this name, and I inquired
of some Indians why the place had been so
called. They replied that their old men had
given it this name, but they did not know the
reason. On this point it may be remembered
that Reuben had four sons, Hanoch, Phailie,
Hezron, and Carmi. How is it that the Indians have given the river the name of Essolon if they had never heard of it? It is not
likely that it was by chance, but much more
probably because it was the custom of the
Jews to carry with them the name of their
estates, or to give their own names to lands
which were in their possession.

The Ottawa and Huron wear their hair
very short, for they say that in this way they
give their enemies less to take hold of. They
leave a tuft on the top of the head, like the
Mahometans. In all matters of importance
the Hurons nearly always speak in the name

of Sataresky, as if he were their true King. The Ottawa are not jealous of their wives, still less are the Huron; and the women are absolutely the mistresses, so that the men hardly do anything without their consent. They think nothing of changing their husbands or, without changing them, of sleeping with anyone they choose. This does not disturb their husbands, who say they are mistresses of their bodies and can dispose of them as they wish; so that it may be said of this tribe that the women and children are held in common, as they were in Lacedemonia. The Huron are friendly with the Ottawa only through necessity, because they are the weaker, having been killed and maltreated to such an extent by the other tribes. They generally make war on the Iroquois, the Sioux, and the tribes in the south, beyond the Illinois.

Let us now see what tribes live around Lake Michigan, which is adjacent to Lake Huron and connected with it. As I have made a map of all these lakes, which in fact are but one, and have marked the number of leagues from one place to another, it seems needless to repeat them here.[11]

[11] If this map could be found it would constitute an excellent addition to our present publication of the Memoir.

I will begin with the Beaver Islands. There are a few families encamped there, who have fields of Indian corn.

The Island of the Poues is still inhabited by the Potawatomi; the reason we call them the Poues is because the first syllable of their name is pronounced so.[12] This tribe is very warlike; they are enemies of the Iroquois and often make successful attacks on them. They show no fear of anyone, although their numbers are smaller than those of many other tribes. Their island produces good crops of grain and the climate is very temperate.

The Noquet tribe is now overthrown; there are so few of them left that they are not entitled to any distinctive name, since they are incorporated in a number of other tribes.[13]

---

[12] The cluster of Islands at the entrance to Green Bay were long known as the Potawatomi Islands. Here the early French explorers first encountered the Potawatomi tribe, many of whose members still live in northern Wisconsin and a few on the Beaver Islands. In 1816 when the detachment of the American army led by Colonel Chambers sailed from Mackinac to establish Fort Howard on the site of Green Bay City, its leader arrogated to himself the privilege of an original discoverer, giving his own name to Chambers Island and that of Washington to the principal island of the Potawatomi group, alluded to in the present Memoir.

[13] Their memory is still preserved in the names of Big and Little Bays de Noc, the northern extension of Green Bay.

The Menominee or Folles Avoines are so called from the river[14] on which their village is situated, where the land produces an enormous quantity of wild rice, which they reap and harvest as we do wheat. They boil it with game or with grease. It is a wholesome food. There is no other tribe whose men are so well-built or so graceful. They are not as swarthy as the others, and if they did not grease themselves they would be whiter than the French. Their women also are very pretty, and more humane than those of their neighbors.

The Sauk tribe is so called because Sauky means the mouth of the river. This tribe is warlike,[15] and they harass the Iroquois. They

[14] The Menominee River, at whose mouth are the twin cities of Menominee, Michigan and Marinette, Wisconsin. The Menominee Indians have never strayed from their eastern Wisconsin homeland of three centuries ago.

[15] The Sauk tribe had formerly lived in eastern Michigan, where their memory is preserved in the names of Saginaw Bay, River, and City. Fleeing before the Iroquois, they found a new home on the lower Fox River of Wisconsin. In the long war between the French and the Foxes which filled much of the first half of the eighteenth century, the Sauk became allied with the latter tribe, and with it were driven westward to find a new home on the upper Mississippi, with their principal village at the mouth of Rock River. Following the Black Hawk War of 1832, waged by one portion of the tribe,

were formerly numerous, but the Illinois, with whom they had several quarrels, surprised them and destroyed a part of the tribe.

The Puans take their name from their river, whose water is very muddy. It is so full of fish of all kinds as to surpass belief, and during the heat of summer, either because of the quality of the water or the excessive numbers of the fish, the water may be seen all covered with them; and as they quickly become putrid one can hardly approach the shore on account of the stench, and consequently the water is disgusting. This is why this tribe is called the Puans (stinkers); for in their persons and habits they are the cleanest men of all the Indians and their women are the least dirty, and take great pains to keep their cabins clean and tidy, a rare accomplishment among the other Indian women.[16]

the surviving remnant of the Sauk and Foxes were removed west of the Missouri River. Several hundred individuals (chiefly Foxes) subsequently returned to Iowa, where their descendants still reside on the only Indian reservation in the heart of the Tall Corn State. The surviving remnants of the Sauk tribe chiefly live in Oklahoma, with a much smaller number in Kansas.

[16] The Puans, or Puants, properly known as the Winnebago, were the first tribe encountered by the French west of Lake Michigan when Nicolet, discoverer of this

The Outagami, or Fox tribe, are so called because they are a cunning and malignant tribe. They are settled on a very fine river in a country that is very good in every way. This tribe is becoming powerful, and for that reason it grows constantly more insolent. I think that if we had not had the war with the Iroquois on our hands, we should have taken steps to humble this tribe, for they have attacked and robbed Frenchmen many

---

lake, made his voyage of 1634 in search of the western ocean and the water route to the Orient. For an account of this undertaking see M. M. Quaife, *Lake Michigan*, Chap. I. Cadillac's explanation of the reason for calling them Puans (meaning stinkers) is but one of several long since advanced. In the Jesuit *Relation* of 1647-48, the Winnebago were called Puants, "not because of any bad odor, that is peculiar to them, but because they say they come from the shores of a far distant sea toward the North, the water of which is salt, they are called the people of the Stinking Water." From their association with Lake Michigan the Jesuits designated this the "Lake of the Stinking Water." The Winnebago continued to reside in Wisconsin until after the Black Hawk War of 1832, when they were forced to remove to a reservation in northeastern Iowa, and subsequently to the borders of the Missouri in South Dakota. Many of the tribe, as individuals, defied the efforts of the government to remove them from Wisconsin, while many others slipped back from their trans-Mississippi reservation to their ancient homeland. In recent decades the surviving Winnebago have lived in about equal numbers in Wisconsin and Nebraska.

times, and treated them shamefully in other ways.[17]

They do not make war on the Iroquois; on the contrary, there is some kind of alliance between them; and it shows the adroitness of this common enemy of all the tribes in the New World that they have succeeded in keeping neutral this one tribe, among all the others, which could have damaged them severely if it had made war upon them. This has been a great help to the Iroquois nation, for by means of the Fox he often devours the hen. When matters are going badly, the Fox Indians intervene with negotiations, and often succeed so well that the Iroquois regain their breath in the interval; for there is no tribe which does not deem itself fortunate and greatly honored to be treated with by an enemy before whom everyone trembles, so that they are never refused peace when they ask for it. But it is always during these negotiations that the Iroquois seize their oppor-

[17] The Outagami (better known by the name of Foxes, given them by the French) closely paralleled in their several removals those of the Sauk tribe, with which they were so long closely allied. The war which Cadillac here foretells broke out at his own Detroit in 1712, and raged, with intervals of inactivity, for three decades, straining the resources of New France to the utmost. For a summary account of the sanguinary struggle see M. M. Quaife, *Lake Michigan*, Chap. 7.

tunity to destroy the tribes which, by some unhappy fate, are always foolish enough to remain idle when their enemy proposes a truce, and all their experience fails to rouse them out of their lethargy. The Foxes are exceedingly dirty, and great thieves, and it is more necessary to watch their feet than their hands, for they use them very cleverly for stealing. They make war on the Sioux and the Chippewa and win many victories over their enemies. They are so little jealous of their daughters that they never refuse them to men who ask for them, if they give them a few trifles.

The post at Chicago comes next. The word means Garlic River, because a very large quantity of garlic grows wild there, without cultivation. There is a village of the Miami there, who are very well-built men; they are good warriors and extremely active; they are veritable greyhounds. They trouble the Iroquois greatly, and are always plucking his hair or feathers. This tribe is numerous, but it is divided into several villages through the jealousy of its chiefs, who cannot get along together, and as they are proud and warlike they make war upon almost all the other tribes. But because they are divided, their enemies defeat them so often that, if they do not re-unite their forces, they run the risk of being completely wiped out. This would be a great pity, for they are fine people, humane and polite, and, as I think, the most inclined to listen to the Gospel tidings.

They are not disturbed by the licentiousness of their daughters, but they are very jealous of their wives and if one of them is convicted of adultery, her husband shaves her head and cuts off her nose and ears and turns her out of his cabin after which she goes where she pleases; and her relatives find nothing to say against it, for such is the law of this tribe. They have another infamous method of punishing adultery. The husband seizes his wife and takes her into the midst of the village; he proclaims in a loud voice the crime of which she is guilty, and invites all the young men to help him punish her. Then he throws her down and is the first to have connection with her. All the others follow suit, sometimes two or three hundred men, who are not disinclined to assist in such a punishment. Usually the guilty woman dies but sometimes she recovers. They maintain that this punishment befits the vice of an unfaithful woman and that, since she is so lustful, it is just that she should be satiated. However, the French have reproached them so much that they seldom inflict this last punishment any more.

Next we find the river of Saint Joseph. There was formerly a fort there, with a French garrison, and there is a village of the same tribe, the Miami.[18] This post is the key of all the tribes bordering the north shore of Lake Michigan, for there are no villages along its southern part, on account of the raids of the Iroquois; but in the back country at the north, and towards the west, there are several, including the Mascouten, . . . Peanguiseins, Peaouarias, Kikapoux, Ayouez, Sioux, and Tintons.

The Sioux are a proud and haughty tribe, who make war on all the others. They excel the Iroquois in valor and courage. They are active, watchful, and cautious and are true warriors. One might say that they sleep with one foot in the air, with a knife always hanging from their wrist. Their bows and quivers serve them for pillows. Unless taken by surprise they are almost invincible, but

[18] This post was established by Count Frontenac in 1691. Its commandant for several years was the Sieur de Courtmanche. The Jesuit mission of St. Joseph was established some years earlier than the fort. The latter was evacuated about 1697 in consequence of the royal decree of May, 1696, requiring the return of all the western garrisons to Lower Canada. For a summary account of both Mission and Post see M. M. Quaife, *Lake Michigan*, Chap. 5. A charming account of the life of the Mission, by Rev. George Paré, is in *Miss. Valley Hist. Review*, XVII, 24-54.

when they are surprised they fight to the death and it is a rare event for a Sioux to be captured alive, for as soon as they see that they can hold out no longer they kill themselves, believing that they are unworthy to live if they are conquered and enslaved.

It is very surprising that men so brave and martial as they are have buckets of tears at their command, such as no one could believe without seeing it. Sometimes you may see them laughing, singing, and amusing themselves; in a moment, you would say that their eyes were rain-spouts, filled by some great storm; and as soon as they cease weeping they revert to their former joy, real or apparent. The chief occasion of their tears is after their enemies have killed some of their warriors, when they address themselves to their allies or to the French commandant. Bowing their heads, they utter horrible howls and shed a deluge of tears, after which they cease their weeping and howling, and their eyes are as dry as if they had not wept at all. They then relate the state of their affairs, so that one might say that they were the same Jews that dwelt on the mountain of Gerizim, who were called the Weepers because they had the gift of tears. There are several lead-mines in the Sioux country, which are very rich.

Chapter 6

THE WESTERN SEA

IN the country of the Sioux there is a river[19] which is known for 1000 leagues around. Its current is gentle and it would carry a ship throughout. It is bordered on both sides by prairies stretching farther than the eye can reach, with a few clumps of trees. Its source is not yet known. The river comes

[19] The Minnesota River, called in Cadillac's time the Saint Peter's. Our author's present chapter undoubtedly contains the best information available at the time it was written concerning the geography of interior North America. The Minnesota, or Saint Peter's River was the Long River of Baron Lahontan's hoax, which for a long time misled the mapmakers. Lahontan's book was first published at The Hague in 1703. If, as we believe, Cadillac's Memoir was written in 1699 or 1700, its statements were obviously not derived from Lahontan's book; and since Cadillac cannot conceivably have been ignorant of any discoveries made by Lahontan, the difference between the latter's Long River tale and the information here set down by Cadillac represents the approximate degree of fiction in Lahontan's Long River story. In short, Cadillac and Lahontan both possessed whatever geographical information was current among Frenchmen in the western country; Cadillac here narrates this truthfully, while Lahontan on the basis of this information elaborated his fictional hoax of pretended Long River discovery.

from the west and joins the Mississippi, which runs into the Southern Sea. It is my belief that the Western Sea could be discovered by means of this river, for experience shows those who travel in this country that every river takes its rise in some lake situated on a mountain or rise of ground which has two slopes, almost always giving rise to two or more rivers. This can easily be seen in Acadia, where one river falls into the sea on the southern side and the other on the northern. Accordingly, those who go to Quebec ascend by lakes or rivers until the land attains a certain height, after which they go continually downwards to the sea.

This observation ought to be general, for in coming from Montreal to the Ottawa country you go up for half the distance or a little more and then at the portage of Varles the river flows down to Lake Nipissing, where it seems to lose itself, and forms the French River which discharges into Lake Huron, over which you can go to Chicago. There a river rises which runs down through the valley of the Mississippi to the Southern Sea; so that one might say that there is a certain height of land near Chicago sloping north and south which divides the water route between the Southern Sea and Quebec, that to the north going through Lake Michigan,

Lake Huron, Lake Erie, and Lake Ontario to Fort Frontenac. This proves clearly enough that nothing is easier than to find a communication between the two seas by way of the lakes and rivers traversing the back country for 1200 or 1500 leagues. By following the Saint Peter's River which empties into the Mississippi, the source of which is to the south-west at 48° latitude and 276° longitude, and which passes through the Sioux country, one can follow it westward for 1000 leagues. Hence, if the Saint Peter's River, which is as large and fine as the Mississippi, takes its rise in some lake situated on some high ground which has two slopes, as is the case with all the other rivers, it is evident that the river on the other slope must fall into the Western Sea, or some other sea, since it is clear that it cannot run into the Eastern Sea, and it is very difficult to imagine that it can possibly flow into the Northern.

We have just said that the source of the Mississippi River is at latitude 48° and longitude 276°. It probably takes its rise in some lake which forms another river going north to fall into the great lake of the Assiniboine,[20] from which spring an endless number

[20] Lake Winnipeg. The Mississippi was long believed to extend far north of its actual source, which was not finally determined until 1832. This error is illustrated

of rivers which have their outfall toward Fort Nelson and in the other great bays. This lake is called by the Indians the grandfather of all the lakes, by which expression they mean that it is incomparably larger than all the others. The Assiniboine report that after traversing the lakes and rivers for 100 days towards the setting sun, you come to the salt sea, beyond which, they say, there is no more land. If this be true, it can only be the western sea.[21]

Finally, it should be observed that one can navigate the interior of the country on fresh water in a ship by proceeding as follows: by building vessels at Fort Frontenac,[22] which can go as far as the Galette, that is, two days' journey from Montreal, and then return to the fort and go by Lake Ontario as far as Niagara. Above the falls other ships must be built, which can go through the river, Lake Erie, and Lake Huron to Sault Saint

by the Treaty of Paris of 1783, which established the present Minnesota-Canadian boundary running westward from Lake Superior and in addition provided that the British should enjoy free navigation of the Mississippi.

[21] This particular geographical puzzle was finally solved by Alexander Mackenzie, whose narrative of his overland journey to the Pacific (*Alexander Mackenzie's Voyage to the Pacific Ocean in 1793*) was reprinted as the Lakeside Classics volume for 1931.

[22] On the site of present-day Kingston, Ontario.

Marie, and from there to Chicago, Green Bay, and the Miamis. Above Sault Saint Marie other ships must be provided to navigate Lake Superior. So that by building a ship on the Mississippi and transporting goods from Chicago to the Mississippi in canoes or wagons and then sailing the ship to the Southern Sea, one can navigate through 2,300 leagues of country, by building vessels in only three places.

Moreover, these are the finest lands ever seen. They are broken by an infinitude of large and beautiful rivers which replenish all the lakes I have mentioned. They are covered with fine virgin forests of elm, walnut, chestnut, oak, cherry, and hazel trees. You see long avenues of apple and plum trees, looking as if they had been planted in lines; vines producing enormous bunches of grapes; beautiful landscapes, and boundless prairies. There are an infinite number of animals there —deer, elk, moose, bears, beavers, and buffaloes weighing 600 to 700 pounds. There is an abundance of small game of all kinds— bustards, geese, ducks, teal, pigeons, partridges, quail, Indian pheasants, and others.

The Illinois tribe is a large one. They are well-made men, as their name clearly shows, for "Illinois" means "real men." They have the same customs as the Miami, and it would therefore be useless to say any more on the subject. Their village is situated on a river which flows into the Mississippi, eight leagues from the fort.[23]

The Mississippi has a large number of tribes on both its banks. The village of the Natchez, however, deserves to be distinguished from the rest, since this tribe is governed by a sovereign whom they obey with great respect and submission. He has a very comfortable dwelling which, as far as the resources of the country permit, has various apartments. No one enters his presence until he has been informed of their coming and has given his permission, which is never granted except to five or six old men, the chiefs of the tribe, who belong to his council.[24]

He alone decides questions of peace or war, and all the important business which concerns the public, and the herald who proclaims his orders does so in these terms: "The Spirit," he says, "makes war and declares it upon such-and-such a tribe. Be ready at such a time," or, in the same way, he makes peace.

[23] The Illinois River. For the village, on Peoria Lake, adjoining Fort Pimatoui see *post*, the Memoir of Liette. The distance from the Mississippi is several times eight leagues.

[24] Since Cadillac at this time had never been on the lower Mississippi this portion of his memoir is evidently based on information obtained from others.

Thus he takes no description or title except that of the Spirit which governs and sets everything in motion. Whatever he orders is never opposed.

He has a body-guard of 100 men who stand as sentries at such posts as he prescribes. When he leaves his house, if anyone wishes to speak to him he kneels on the ground reclining on his elbow, putting his hand before his face, lowering his head, and keeping his eyes fixed on the ground. It is in this posture that they speak to him, to ask for justice or for some favor. The moment he leaves his house the people utter loud shouts and howls, raising their hands toward heaven as if a divinity were showing himself to them. When he goes for a walk he finds his path swept clean, watered, and covered with clean mats, stretched tight and strewn with flowers from one end to the other. He alone walks upon the path; those who follow him walk on either side of it, as if they feared to profane his feet by walking in his footsteps.

He has several wives and concubines, who have their own apartments, and no one is allowed to speak to them nor to visit them. When he dies they slaughter his favorites and those whom he loved most, especially those who have guarded his person, in order, they say, that they may bear him company on his journey; and these simpletons consider their fate a happy one and look upon the fatal choice as a high honor. They even kill the dogs and horses he thought most of.

In the village there is a temple neatly furnished with mats, with a pillar in the middle on which there is a bow and a quiver with various skins and figures of snakes. Towards the middle on the right side there is an altar made of earth with a large earthenware pot with water in it; and near the door there is another altar on which a fire is kept continually by a man appointed for this duty. There is another village four leagues from Natchez called Noema where the daughter of this chief is the ruler and commands with as much authority as her father, and independently of him.

The name of this village has suggested to me that it is Jewish, for Thobel, son of Sella, had an only daughter called Noema. It may be that her descendants have always kept this name, and have held it in veneration, so that for this reason the name of this Jewish lady may have been given to the village; and as she was an only daughter and no doubt dearly loved, it may have been decided for this reason that the eldest daughter of this chief should be the supreme ruler in her village, which is a very large one and almost strong enough to resist the village of Natchez. It is also well to know that this chieftainess bears the name of her village. I am well aware that chance is generally a factor in the giving of names, whether for solid and necessary reasons or even for extravagant reasons; but it must also be acknowledged that there are names which are beautiful only because they have been used ever since they were first originated. So if anyone wishes to say that it is a mere chance that the village of which I have just spoken bears the name of the daughter of Thobel, why should anyone find fault with me for thinking that the village was so named in memory of that girl, to perpetuate her name, especially since everything points to this opinion, and, above all, the custom of always having the eldest daughter of a sovereign for its chief? I call him a sovereign because he is in fact absolute and is respected and obeyed too well for us to refuse him this title.

When the sun rises, all the people come out of their dwellings and, turning towards the beautiful star of day, say their prayers, with their hands uplifted to the sky; but they pray by howling like wolves.

The heads and foreheads of the men are so flat that it would seem their brains would be crushed, and this is their idea of beauty.

They work hard and will not allow their wives to do heavy tasks. The Indian women here may be said to be the least hard-worked of all. Their heads are not flat like those of the men, and they are very pretty and tidy. They are clad like the Egyptian women. They make their cloths and stuffs from the bark of elm trees, which they make into packets or bunches, as we do with hemp. They put them to soak in water for some time, and make them whiter than cotton; with these fibers they make skirts with very pretty embroidery, and of different colors, for they have all sorts of dyes. They wear several tassels on their shoulders such as was formerly the custom in France. Their hair is bound with a ribbon and wound around their heads. In short, they are moderately good-looking. Their country is a land of promise.

Some will perhaps think that we are very unenterprising not to have found out from the tribes we know the reasons for their customs and ceremonies and various other matters of which I speak with diffidence, but it is not so easy as might be thought, for sometimes it happens that the Indians themselves know nothing about them, or that travelers have not the gift of learning their language, so that they can neither express what they want to say nor understand clearly what the

Indians wish to tell them, so that there is difficulty on both sides. Moreover they are barbarous and malicious people, and it is not prudent to question them too closely at the first interviews. The only way is to humor them at first and then gradually make them tractable, for which there is no better method than by associating and conversing with them, but this stage is not to be reached at one bound. You cannot gain a knowledge of so many different languages in a day. It is much to be able to talk to them sufficiently for what is absolutely necessary for attaining the purpose you have in view.

Memoir of Pierre Liette on
the Illinois Country

The Memoir of
Pierre Liette
—

THE Illinois country is undeniably the finest that is known anywhere between the mouth of the St. Lawrence River and that of the Mississippi, which are a thousand leagues apart. You begin to see its fertility at Chicago which is 140 leagues from Michilimackinac, at the end of Lake Michigan. The Chicago is a little river only two leagues long bordered by prairies of equal width. This is the route usually taken to go to this country. At this river a portage is made, of a quarter of a league in low water and of an arpent in high water.[1] A tiny stream half a league long issues from two little lakes that extend a league and a half, at the end of which, on the rising ground at this point, a short portage simply of one's baggage is made. When the water is favorable you re-

---

[1] The *arpent*, or acre, was a measure employed by the French to indicate both length and area. The linear measure was equal to slightly less than 193 English feet. The French acre was a square area whose sides were an arpent each.

embark at once, but when it is low you must carry it a league.

This is called the Portage of the Oaks; and it requires much effort to propel the boat in this streamlet, which empties into the river which the French call the Illinois.[2] However, this is not the Illinois, as we only come to that stream twenty leagues farther on. The passage is very difficult on account of the low waters which render this river virtually impracticable, since travellers ordinarily reach this region only in summer or autumn. There are ten places where for half a league it is necessary to take out half of the baggage, and very often to remove it entirely, until the deep water is reached. Sometimes you are also compelled to carry the canoe. There is even a place called Mount Joliet, where there are four leagues of rapids, and where this must almost always be done.

[2] The modern Des Plaines River. Present-day usage regards the Illinois as beginning at the confluence of the Des Plaines and the Kankakee. The memoir discloses that Liette regarded the Kankakee as the continuation of the Illinois and the Des Plaines as a tributary of the latter river. For modern descriptions of the Chicago Portage see M. M. Quaife, *Chicago and the Old Northwest* (Chicago, 1913), Chap. I and Robert Knight and Lucius H. Zeuch, *The Location of the Chicago Portage Route of the Seventeenth Century* (Chicago, 1928). The most vivid description of the Portage and its hazards ever written is contained in *The Autobiography of Gordon Saltonstall Hubbard*.

This place is called Illes, because a voyageur who had that name was detained here a long time. The Illinois and Miami call it Missouratenouy, which signifies an earthen vessel. Indeed it has some resemblance to one; it is about three arpents long and half an arpent wide. It is embanked as if it had been purposely shaped, and is about thirty feet high, situated an eighth of a league from the river in a very beautiful valley. The woods on the other side are distant about three arpents; there is only one tree on it. Several Illinois and Miami have tried to persuade me that at the time of the deluge, of which it appears they have learned, it was a vessel which had been made to save all mankind from shipwreck; and that, on the subsiding of the waters, being on a bad bottom, it had upset, and in course of time it had changed to earth.[3]

---

[3] Mount Joliet, standing isolated in an otherwise level plain, excited the interest of all early travelers. Henry R. Schoolcraft, who visited and described it in 1820, notes that it was then about 600 yards west of the "present" channel of the Des Plaines, but immediately upon what appeared to be the former bank of the river. Schoolcraft's figures (estimated) for the dimensions of the mound differ curiously from those of Liette, making it much larger in area and twice as high. For his description see *Pictures of Illinois One Hundred Years Ago*, the Lakeside Classics volume for 1918, pp. 115–16.

Here you generally begin to see the buffalo. As for turkeys, there are quantities of them. There is a game bird that is abundant which is a good deal like the French pheasant, and which is very good. Formerly it was found at Chicago, but since a band of Miami settled there these birds have gone farther off. Four leagues from here is the fork of the real river of the Illinois, which has its source two leagues above the village of the Miami of the St. Joseph River, whence it flows always northward for 120 leagues up to the fork.[4] Afterwards it bends to the southwest and empties into the Mississippi.

Here you begin to see the beauty of this country, both for the soil, which yields bounti-

[4] The Kankakee, here characterized, takes its rise near South Bend, Indiana, at which place was the formerly notable St. Joseph-Kankakee Portage. The Miami village on the St. Joseph was at present-day Niles, some half dozen miles down-river from the Portage. The Kankakee flows in a general southwesterly direction from its source to the city of Kankakee, where it turns northwesterly to its junction with the Des Plaines. It is this latter portion, only, of the river to which Liette's "northward" applies. Evidently he was more familiar with the Des Plaines and the Illinois than he was with the Kankakee. Much the best account of the St. Joseph Mission is Rev. George Paré's "The St. Joseph Mission" in *Miss. Valley Hist. Rev.*, XVII, 24–54. For the St. Joseph Baptismal Register see *Ibid.*, XIII, 211–39.

fully, and for the abundance of animals. On one side you see prairies requiring only to be turned up by the plow, and on the other side valleys spreading half a league before reaching the hills, covered with walnuts and oaks; and behind these, prairies like those I have just spoken of. Sometimes you travel a league, seeing all this from your boat. Afterwards you find virgin forests on both sides, consisting of tender walnuts, ash, whitewood, Norway maple, cottonwood, a few maples, and grass, taller in places than a man. More than an arpent in the woods you find marshes which in autumn and spring are full of bustards, swans, ducks, cranes, and teals. Ten steps farther on are the hills covered with wood extending about an eighth of a league, from the edge of which are seen prairies of extraordinary extent. Three leagues from the fork is the river Mazon, which signifies the tow, where flocks of parakeets of fifty to sixty are found. They make a very strange noise. They are a little bigger than turtle-doves.

Seven leagues from here is a rapid where, in low water, you have to portage for an eighth of a league. Three leagues farther are some places that are very flat because of several islands that are located here, and a river flowing from the north, which the Illinois call

Pestequouy.[5] Near its outlet there is a rich quarry of coal. This river comes from the northeast. It has nothing but prairies on either side, except for a narrow strip of wood consisting of oaks and walnuts, and running the whole length of its banks.

From here it is two leagues to the old fort. This is a steep rock, very favorably situated, which induced the late Monsieur de la Salle to build a fort here in 1682 or 1683.[6] As I was not yet in the country I do not know the exact date. I did not arrive until 1687.

It was very easy for me, in view of my extreme youth, to learn the language of this nation. There were also a hundred families of Shawnee. But, aside from the fact that I never saw them except for two years, I had so little inclination for their language, and so great a desire to know that of the Illinois, that I learned very little of it. What attracted me still more was that I was told that the languages of the Illinois and of the Miami were the same, and this is true, there being

[5] Present-day Fox River, which joins the Illinois at Ottawa. The discovery of coal deposits in this vicinity was evidently made very early by the French explorers of Illinois. Other earlier names for Fox River were Rock, and Buffalo River.

[6] Fort St. Louis on Starved Rock, established by La Salle in 1682 and abandoned, as our diarist subsequently relates, by command of Tonty in 1691.

no difference except that the accent of the
Illinois is very short and that of the Miami
very long. One pronounces the *h* and the
other the *f*.

This was my reason, in 1688, for begging
Monsieur de Tonty to allow me to accompany a village of Illinois who were going off
on a buffalo hunt for five weeks. He readily
granted this request, being pleased to have
me learn this language, for which he saw I
had some liking, that he might safely absent
himself when his affairs demanded it, and
leave me in his place. He recommended me
to the chief of this village, and with my servant I was placed in a cabin of savage men,
if one may say that there are any men among
barbarians.

We went into camp two leagues away. As
I saw only old men, women, and girls, and
five or six young men, I asked them, partly
with the few words that I knew and partly
by signs, how it happened that there were so
few young men. They told me that they
were out on a hunting expedition. The women
had thrown down their packs and had run,
each with an axe, into the woods to cut poles
and to peel bark for their summer hunting
cabin. As for the kind they use during their
winter sojourn, they always carry these
along; they are similar to those which they

have in summer, as I shall tell in the proper place. They set them up on the edge of a prairie so as to be in a cool place, for in the month of June and in order to be in the open all the southern nations establish themselves in the most open spots so as to see what is going on, and so as not to be taken by surprise, and in case an attack is made upon them, so as to be able to pursue.

While the women and girls were making the cabins the few young men who were with us went an arpent into the woods to cut three poles with which they made a large tripod from which they hung a big kettle, which they filled with water and then seated themselves around the fire which they had made underneath. My man and I settled down near them. A short time afterward two men arrived, each with a buck on his back. Two of our cooks went to meet them. Upon seeing them approach, the hunters threw down their load and advanced proudly toward us, highly elated at being the first to bring meat to the camp. Our servitors soon had the bucks cut up and put into the kettle. When they were cooked the old men were called and came to eat. We were the first served and got the best there was.

I noticed that this happened every day, and that some young men always came by turns with the old men. They are called guards, and they prevent anyone from separating from the band and going off alone, because this frightens away the game. A man and a woman once tried to escape from the band while the guards were busy gathering strawberries. One of the guards saw them and ran after them, took away the man's load, cut the collar and the bear skins which they used as a mattress, smashed the kettles which the woman was carrying, and came near killing a child, which she had upon her load, by pulling it from her head; and all this happened without the man or woman saying a single word.

The next day we saw in a prairie a great herd of buffaloes. A halt was called and two old men harangued the young men for half an hour, urging them to show their skill in shooting down all the buffaloes that we saw, and to manage so as to make all those that they could not kill move toward us. After removing us to the nearest spot, they started out in two bands, running always at a trot. When they were about a quarter of a league from the animals they all ran at full speed, and when within gunshot they fired several volleys and shot off an extraordinary number of arrows. A great number of buffaloes remained on the ground, and they pursued the rest in such a manner that they were driven toward us. Our old men butchered these.

As for me, I did not shoot. Their appearance filled me with terror, and I withdrew from our band when I saw them approach. This set all the savages laughing, at which I was not a little mortified. Those animals are certainly frightful looking beasts and they usually terrify people who have never seen them.

The cows are as big as big oxen are here. They have a hump about eight inches high which extends from their shoulders to the middle of their backs. Their entire heads are covered with fine hair so that their eyes can hardly be seen. They have short hair in summer, but from September until June they are covered with a very fine wool.

To return to the hunt in which our savages engaged, they killed 120 buffaloes, from which they brought back a hundred tongues. The people from my cabin smoked these and distributed them among themselves to carry to me.

We remained a week in this place in order to dry all this meat. For this purpose they make a kind of cradle ten feet long, three feet wide, and four feet high, which they call *gris*, upon which they spread out their meat after preparing it. Under this they kindle a little fire. It usually takes them a day to dry a flat side. There are two of these in a buffalo. They take it from the shoulder clear to the thigh and from the hump to the middle of the belly, after which they spread it out as thin as they can, usually making it four feet square. They fold it up while still hot, like a portfolio, so as to make it easier to carry. The strongest men and women carry as many as eight for a whole day. This is not possible in autumn nor in winter, however, as the cows are then very fat; they can then carry four at most.

The drying of this meat by the women and girls does not prevent the young men from going to the chase every day each for himself, for it is only when they all go together that they have guards. If anyone has no luck (which rarely happens in buffalo hunting), his relatives contribute from their share. These little hunts are ordinarily for bucks, bears, and young turkeys, on which they feast, not failing to invite the strangers whom they have among them (a very frequent thing), such as Miami, Ottawa, Potawatomi, Kickapoo, and others; so that there were days when I was invited as many as ten times. We did not dare to refuse, having learned that they were grieved if anyone who was among them did not come.

Some days later they again surrounded a large herd of buffaloes. I went to the chase in the hope of finding one of these isolated, so as to surprise and kill him and thus redeem in some measure the poor opinion they had formed of me because of the fear I had shown at the sight of the first buffaloes. About an eighth of a league from the spot where we were camping I heard a loud breathing in the brushwood. I listened intently, and having assured myself that I was not mistaken, I advanced as softly as I could and saw a calf stretched on the ground, its mother having been killed. It was completely exhausted. I did not wait long to shoot it. Several women who were in the vicinity, engaged in peeling off bark, came up on hearing the report. One of them, leaving the others, went off to the village to announce that I had killed a calf. Two old men came up, who told me that the animal was not worth the shot, as the calves are never fat, but as this was the first animal that I had killed they felt it must be given the proper honors. They skinned it, leaving nothing but the entrails and the skin, and as soon as all our hunters had returned one of the old men went off to harangue the village, announcing that I had killed a calf and that they must partake of it, in order to thank the Master of Life because he had allowed me to begin to kill game. The meat was divided among 120 men, who did not allow the least scrap of it to be wasted. We did not taste it, as it is not customary for the savages to eat when they give a feast.

The same day I assembled the old men in our cabin and gave them all the powder and bullets that we had, telling them that since we were not able to kill game while pursuing it on the run, I wished them to divide it with the young men, as it was not fair that they should feed us for nothing; and I told the inmates of our own cabin that I should find a way to reward them according to the good treatment they accorded us. We perceived that they had understood me by the extraordinary care they took of us when we were on the march. If we showed signs of being thirsty, the most agile of them ran to fetch water for us from places that we should never have discovered.

As regards thirst, having gone to the chase, I found two men in a prairie who were skinning a buffalo. They told me to come with them as they wanted to have me eat a broiled slice of their meat. I told them I needed a drink more than food. They said that no water was to be found except at a great distance, but that there was some in the buffalo which they had killed not half an

hour before, if I would have a little patience.
I thought I had not rightly understood them,
and the savages, perceiving this, said nothing in reply to everything that I said to them
except, "Wait." My thirst was not so great
but that I could do so, but I was apprehen-
sive about the two leagues and more that
remained to be traversed before arriving at
the woods, where streams are to be found.
They hurried as much as they could in skinning their buffalo, and I helped them lay it
on its back. After opening its belly, they
opened the paunch and separated with their
hands the excrements from the water which
had not yet had time to be absorbed. Using
my hands, I drank as much as I wished. It
had a bad taste, but in spite of this I had the
pleasure of slaking my thirst.

When I came for the broiled meat on
which they had promised to feast me, I could
not understand where they would get means
for cooking it. They took a fillet from within
the body, this being the most tender part in
all sorts of animals, and cut it into strips like
sausages. One of them went off three or four
arpents into a hollow, which in spring is nothing but a sort of marsh, and brought back a
bundle of round reeds as thick as one's fingers.
They drew from their quivers two bits of
wood which serve them for striking a flame,

and in almost no time they had a fire. They
kindled a part of their reeds, over which they
put their meat, which they turned from time
to time with their bows. In spite of all the
care they took to scrape it with their knives
some ash remained, which rendered it as
black as itself. Nevertheless, I ate heartily
and found it very good. It was very tender
and I had a good appetite.

One of the pieces of wood which they use
to make a fire is of white cedar, which is the
most combustible, a foot long more or less,
according as they choose to make it, and as
thick as two fingers. On one side, on the very
edge, they make little holes, in which they
make a notch. They put this bit of wood on
some rotten wood or on some grass, dry and
very fine, after taking care to crush it thoroughly in their hands. The other piece of
wood is as thick as the little finger; it is a bit
of a wood that has a black berry, which we
call *morette*. When this wood is green it is
very soft, and it is proportionately hard when
it is dry. They shape the end to the size of
the holes in the other piece of wood, into one
of which they insert it, and by turning it in
their hands without ceasing, they produce a
sort of powder from which, after a very short
time, one sees smoke issue, which shortly is
converted into flame. This, coming through

the notch of which I have just spoken, falls on the rotten wood or dry grass, which is ignited.

We went as much as twenty leagues from the fort on this hunt, and I may say truthfully that no finer landscape can be found. There are avenues extending farther than the eye can reach, which seem made expressly by nature to provoke our admiration, and offering, though about as wide as the Cours de la Reine, not a single bit of brushwood. This may be due to the endless number of buffaloes that pass there. The reason why these places are so much frequented by these animals is because there is a kind of marsh here and there in the middle of these runways which serves them for watering places.

More than 1,200 buffaloes were killed during our hunt, without counting the bears, does, stags, bucks, young turkeys, and lynxes. We also killed some animals which the Illinois and Miami call *Quinousaoueia*, which signifies the big tails, as they have tails more than two feet long, a head like that of a cat, a body about three feet long, a very lank belly and long legs, and fur, reddish and very short. They move faster than any other beast for two or three arpents. If they were as common as wolves we should not see so many bucks in that country, for they live only on these.

I saw an exploit of a young man of about twenty-two years which will show the agility of these savages, and which made me admire him and gave great pleasure to a thousand people, themselves trained runners. On returning to the fort we saw on a large prairie in which we were (for these people have lynx-eyes) a band of about sixty does quite near the wood which we were about to enter. Several young men started off, part to the right, part to the left, and when they arrived in the wood opposite the place where they had seen them, they made for the animals and reached the prairie, with part of our people behind them and with others on their flanks. They chased them for half an hour, letting them go now to one side, now to the other, but steering them continually toward us. The youth of whom I wish to speak as the most agile outran his comrades and caught up with the animals, laying his hand on the back of one of them while uttering cries of victory. Afterwards he drew several arrows from his quiver, with which he killed and wounded several. Those who had remained behind, like ourselves, ran up, and we killed more than half of them with our guns. We camped in the wood where we had seen them, and came back from there to get the meat.

We found in these woods a vast number of trees laden with medlars, and others with nuts which have a wonderfully delicate taste. They are ordinarily olive-shaped but twice as big. The shells are very thin. There is a testa inside dividing the kernel in two, which is very bitter. There were other trees as thick as one's leg, which bend under a yellowish fruit of the shape and size of a medium-sized cucumber, which the savages call *assemina*. The French have given it an impertinent name. Some people would not like it, but I find it very good. They have five or six nuclei inside which are as big as marsh beans, and of about the same shape. One day I ate sixty of them, big and little. This fruit does not ripen till October, like the medlars.

Grapes grow here in such abundance that one cannot travel four arpents without finding trees full of trellises of charming beauty, with clusters sometimes as large as those in France, but most of them have the berries far apart. I cannot say as much of their quality, for of all those I have tasted, I have found none that are edible. I tried to cook some and used more than a quarter of a pound of sugar to a pint of this juice, yet it was impossible for me or my servant to swallow it.

There are wood rats here as big as a French cat, which have white fur inclining to red-

dish, as long as that of a marten. It is very
fine and the women make garters of it. They
have tails a foot long and as thick as a finger,
just like that of the muskrat. The female has
two skins under her belly which gives the
effect of a cloak closed at the top and the bottom and open in the middle. They have as
many as eight young, which they carry inside when they walk.

Some savages brought me a couple of them
once during the winter. I hoped to send them
to France, but I was surprised some days
afterward to find their tails missing. The
cold had frozen them and they had broken
off like glass. Sometime later their ears also
dropped off, so that I was obliged to kill them.
Some savages to whom I told this informed
me that the mothers always kept them in
their holes until they were as big as themselves, and that they never went out when it
was very cold. They are very good to eat.
They are very heavy, and there is no need of
running after them for when they see anyone
they do not flee. They only open their
mouths and you smash their heads with a
stick.

There is also a great abundance of stinking animals who produce an infectious stench
with the smell of their urine. This is their
defense. When one tries to approach them

to kill them, they immediately turn tail and urinate if they can. The dogs, after having strangled them, are often like mad for a very long time. They do all they can by rolling on the ground to get rid of this bad smell, which sticks to them for a long time. This does not keep the savages from making dresses of their skins, the fur being white and black and very warm. The meat is very tender, but despite all precautions taken in washing it, it develops an unpleasant odor when eaten.

Plums are also very abundant here, and not inferior in beauty to those of France. I once found some which were no different in appearance from our *Imperiale*, but they had a very different flavor. They are never freestone, and have a very thick skin. There are also in the prairies many orchards whose trees are laden with apples as big as the Api, but very bad. I was never able to eat them except after boiling them or after they had been frozen.

We got back from our hunt toward the middle of July. From that time until the end of September bands of ten, fifteen, and twenty Illinois arrived continually, to the number of 800. The late Monsieur de Tonty had sent them out at the beginning of March against the Iroquois, by order of the Marquis Denonville.[7] They brought in this summer, captive or killed, sixty men, women, and children.

In the autumn Monsieur de la Forest[8] arrived, who told us that the Iroquois had killed many of the French and that everybody was in great dismay. He and Monsieur de Tonty used all their address to induce as many Illinois as possible to set out against them. In this they were fairly successful, for the following summer [1688] we burned six Iroquois, and they brought in more than twenty scalps.

In 1691 Monsieur de Tonty left for some business which he had at Michilimackinac, leaving me to take command in his place.

---

[7] The allusion is to the invasion of the Iroquois country by Denonville in 1687. Tonty, Duluth and other leaders were ordered to rouse the western Indians and lead them to a rendezvous with the main army from Montreal, appointed for Irondequoit Bay, from which base the real invasion of the Seneca country was launched. Although some minor successes were achieved the campaign on the whole resulted in dismal failure. Another year or two of blundering brought New France to the verge of utter ruin, to forefend which Count Frontenac was sent out to begin his second term as Governor.

[8] Francois Daupin de la Forest was a captain of troops, an associate of La Salle, and long the partner of Henry de Tonty in the Illinois country. At a later date he succeeded Cadillac as commandant at Detroit, retaining this position until his death in 1714. For his career see *Michigan Pioneer Colls.*, XXXIV, 308–10.

Before his departure he assembled all the principal Illinois and told them that he was leaving me in his place, and that in case any matters turned up regarding the service of the king or the well-being of their village they had only to apply to me—he would approve whatever I might do. I learned afterward that this speech had had no little effect on their minds, for I can truthfully say to their credit that never had they been so submissive as they were during this time.

Some of the women complained that their corn had been cut, and others that they had found Iroquois moccasins in their fields. I assembled the principal Indians, whom I feasted on a flat side of buffalo, and told them that they should remember that Monsieur de Tonty had bid them listen to me whenever I might have something to tell them concerning the safety of their wives and children. I told them that I was informed that there were enemies out against them who were cutting their corn, and that these might be a band of Iroquois who were coming among them as they had done in the past. I said it was my opinion that they ought to send out scouts on the roads over which they knew they were likely to come, as undoubtedly, if it was true, as their women said, that enemies had cut their corn, they would surprise the enemy scouts, who doubtless were waiting for the crop to ripen before attacking them.

They approved of my idea, and that very night sent out four bands of twenty men each who four days later brought in two Iroquois who had cut corn for the last time. They numbered 300 men. This made them draw back, happily for the Illinois, for at that time there were not 200 young men in the village. As soon as they were brought in they were fastened to the stake. I had only three men with me at the time, the Reverend Father Gravier being a fifth. Soon after this several bands of the men whom Monsieur de Tonty had sent out in the spring came in. They brought in four more prisoners whom we also burned. Our Illinois lost four of their number, at which we were greatly pleased because this roused them still more.

In September I received a letter from Monsieur de Tonty, dated at Michilimackinac, informing me that he had learned that Monsieur de la Forest was returning from France and that the Court had granted them the country of the Illinois with the same prerogatives as the late Monsieur de la Salle. He said he was returning with a large number of *engagés*, and that I should therefore sound the Illinois regarding the abandonment of their village, for which they had shown a desire because their firewood was so remote and because it was so difficult to get water upon the Rock if they were attacked by the enemy. I assembled the chiefs, and having learned that they had not changed their minds, I bade them choose such place as suited them best. They chose the end of Lake Pimitoui, which means Fat Lake, so called on account of the abundance of game there.

This is where the Illinois are at present and where I was for seven years. Monsieur de Tonty arrived in the winter [1691–1692] and started the building of a large fort to which the savages might retire in case of an alarm.[9] The following spring Monsieur de la Forest also arrived with a considerable number of *engagés* and of soldiers who completed the building of it. It is four years ago this spring that I left the place. I left there something over 260 cabins, which have from one to four

[9] The fort, sometimes called St. Louis but commonly Pimitoui, was on the north side of Lake Peoria in or very close to the present city of Peoria. It "was surrounded by 1800 pickets, had two large log houses, one for lodgings and one for a warehouse, and, to shelter the soldiers, two other houses built of uprights." Around it settlers soon collected to form the first permanent village in Illinois. See C. W. Alvord, *The Illinois Country, 1673–1818*, 100.

fires. I put them at two on the average, and thus calculate about 800 warriors between the ages of twenty and forty.

You can see no finer looking people. Usually they are neither tall nor short; there are some you could encompass with your two hands. They have legs that seem drawn with an artist's pen. They carry their load of wood gracefully, with a proud gait, as finely as the best dancer. They have faces as beautiful as white milk, in so far as this is possible for Indians of that country. They have the most regular and the whitest teeth imaginable. They are full of life, yet at the same time lazy. They are tattooed behind from the shoulders to the heels, and as soon as they have reached the age of twenty-five, on the front of the stomach, the sides, and the upper arms. There is a Frenchman here named Villeneuve, who has half his back tattooed in the same manner.

They are proud and vain and all call themselves sons or relatives of chiefs; but in spite of this they are given to begging, are cowardly, licentious, and entirely given up to their senses. They always take advantage of the weakness of those they deal with. They dress their best when they appear in public. They are as jealous as Italians, thievish, gourmands ,vindictive, hypocritical, and perfidious. They would prostitute their daughters or sisters a thousand times for a pair of stockings or other trifle. I have got men to agree a hundred times that their fathers, their brothers, and their children were worse than dogs, because they hoped that I would give them a little red paint or a five-cent knife.

The sin of sodomy prevails more among them than in any other nation, although there are four women to one man. It is true that the women, although debauched, retain some moderation, which prevents the young men from satisfying their passions as much as they would like. There are men who are bred for this purpose from their childhood. When they are seen frequently picking up the spade, the spindle, the axe, but making no use of the bow and arrows, as all the other small boys do, they are girt with a piece of leather or cloth which envelops them from the belt to the knees, a thing all the women wear. Their hair is allowed to grow and is fastened behind the head. They also wear a little skin like a shoulder strap passing under the arm on one side and tied over the shoulder on the other. They are tattooed on their cheeks like the women and also on the breast and the arms, and they imitate their accent, which is different from that of the men. They omit nothing that can make them like the

women. There are men sufficiently embruted
to have dealings with them on the same foot-
ing. The women and girls who prostitute
themselves to these wretches are dissolute
creatures.

Formerly a man had to make several
attacks on the enemy before he could marry,
a thing he did not do until he was at least
twenty-five, the period when a man begins
to possess resolution, so that they were really
about thirty when they married. The girls
also waited till they were twenty-five. At
present there are men who do not wait till
they are twenty, and girls marry under
eighteen. The old men say that the French
have corrupted them.

When a young man has succeeded in learning to hunt, he tells his father that he wishes
to marry and names the girl he loves, to
whom sometimes he has never spoken, for a
chaste girl among the Illinois as well as among
the Miami ought not to hold any conversation with the young men, nor even with the
married men. When they speak of marriage,
she must never speak to them first, nor cast
her eyes upon them, for as soon as a young
man notices that a girl looks at him frequently and afterwards whispers to some
one of her companions, he conjectures that
she is in love with him, and usually he is not

mistaken. He therefore neglects no opportunity to take advantage of this, and spies out the time when she goes to the woods or to her field. He begs her to listen to him, and assures her of his love. The girl, half overcome already, does not answer a word, which is an infallible sign among them that she loves him. He appoints a rendezvous with her and sometimes obtains without delay all that he desires. Accordingly a really well-conducted girl should avoid gatherings where men are present, in order to be esteemed and married with ceremony. This is done in the following manner.

It is usually at the time when the young man is absent either making war or hunting. His father, if he has one, or his uncle in lieu of him, takes five or six kettles, two or three guns, some skins of stags, bucks, or beavers, some flat sides of buffaloes, some cloth, and sometimes a slave, if he has one, in short something of all he has, according to his wealth and the esteem in which the girl is held. He has these presents delivered by his female relatives, who deposit them in the cabin of the girl, who goes out as soon as she is aware that the presents have been brought for her, and he merely says to the father or to her nearest relatives that he asks his alliance and that he begs him to have pity on him and to suffer him to warm himself at his fire. They use this expression because it is always the women who supply the cabins and the firewood. They also say that they come to seek moccasins, because it is the women also who dress the skins.

Sometimes the presents remain in the cabin for four days without any answer being given, on account of the objections made by the girl, who does not like the boy, or on account of her brother who is in favor of some other suitor, who perhaps has been seeking his good graces for a long time by means of little presents, so that he may favor him in the same matter, which he has not yet been able to arrange, either through lack of merchandise or because his relatives are absent. In such a case the presents are returned and nothing is said. The father of the youth, knowing how much his son is bent on marrying this girl, augments the presents and returns to her home, saying that it is at her fire only that he wishes to warm himself. I have seen presents carried back as many as three times. This often produces discouragement, and they address themselves to other girls for whom they have heard their sons express esteem.

In the end, therefore, the girl and her brother consent, on account of the suasion of the father and mother, who extol the good qualities of the youth. For this reason, in accordance with the means of the girl, they carry back several things resembling those that were brought to them, and the girl marches ahead well adorned with shoulder straps, glass beads, porcelain, and bells, so that to one who hears them marching they seem like mules. They spread a bear skin, or that of a buffalo or a stag, according to the season, in the middle of the cabin, on which they seat the bride, and the relatives who followed her carrying the presents return home. In the evening the relatives of the youth bring her back with some presents. This is usually done as many as four successive days. The last day she remains. There are some who wait for the bridegroom's return before going there for the last time.

They sometimes remain a whole week without approaching each other. It has happened that men, getting angry at being too long rebuffed by their wives, have left them and gone off to war without having known them, and have been killed. Sometimes this happens because they do not love their husbands, at other times to do themselves honor, for when they have children immediately at the end of nine months it is a matter of reproach when they quarrel to say that they loved their husbands before marrying them, since they had borne children so soon. I knew one woman who assured me that she and her husband had lived together six months without having intercourse.

When such accidents occur these women are to be pitied, for the relatives of the man continually reproach her with his death. They dare not comb their hair nor be present at any dance, still less can they marry. They are obliged to live very quietly in spite of themselves, often shedding many tears until the relatives are finally moved to pity. The sister combs her, and urges her to marry if she finds some suitor. To show them the regret that she feels and her gratitude toward them, she must remain a year without marrying. If, unhappily for her, she were to do so before it was allowed, the relatives of the deceased would lift her scalp as if she were one of their enemies, and would put it into a hoop and hang it at the end of a pole at the top of their cabin. When they are faithless to their husbands the same treatment is accorded them. The husband or the relatives do not wait for an opportune moment, but no matter where they find the woman outside of her cabin they take the law into their own hands.

The Miami cut off their noses. Others inflict another punishment. They post about thirty young men on a road along which they know their wives must pass in going to the woods. As soon as they see her, the husband issues from the ambuscade and says to his wife: As I know that you are fond of men, I offer you a feast of them—take your fill. Her cries are futile; several of them hold her, and they enjoy her one after the other. There are even some men who are always present on such occasions.

I was chagrined to see this happen one day in our fort, where I was in command at the time. A chief who was one of my friends came to tell me that he knew that at the very moment he was talking to me his wife was locked up with my servant in the house opposite mine, where he cooked for me. He added that but for the respect he had for me he would do an ill turn to that Frenchman. He begged me to tell him to take care lest this happen again, and added that not all men would show as much regard for me. He asked me to come with him to have the door opened, which had been kept closed in spite of much knocking on his part and of many invitations from him to open it. So I went there with him, and the Frenchman still kept us waiting so long that I scolded him for being so slow to answer my calls. He finally opened the door and the woman came out holding in her hands a piece of paper containing some vermilion. Her husband laid hold of her and led her off to one of the bastions of our fort, where there were twenty young men who did not spare her.

Others, who are braver, inflict wounds on the lover with knives or arrows, of which he sometimes dies. When he is merely wounded his relatives say nothing; but if he dies his brothers or her nearest relatives take vengeance on the one who dealt the blow or on his brothers, in spite of all the presents that are given to appease them. Ordinarily blankets, kettles, guns, and slaves are given for this purpose. There are some men who say that the women are not worth the price of the least resentment, and that when they prove faithless one should be content to drive them away and take others.

Since I have been in this country more than a hundred women have been scalped. It is true that the young men can easily rouse their love for, as I have already said, they are the handsomest Indians that I know, good hunters, good runners, intelligent, affecting great generosity toward the brothers of the women they love, who encourage their sisters to return their love, although married women. When, in addition to all this, they are warriors, there are few who do not succumb to them. The women are rather ugly than beautiful, tolerably fair for savages, and quite cleanly. They always bend one leg inward on which they sit when they are taking on a load. Those who are tall and slender are the most beautiful. Thus when Madame LeSueur, who is very tall and slender, very blonde, and who has a well-shaped face, came among the Illinois she was much admired and was obliged to pass two entire days outside the fort. Otherwise my house would not have been left standing because of the number of people bent on seeing her.[10]

In this connection, the wife of a man of standing, the mother-in-law of one of our Frenchmen, gave me an answer which does not seem to me quite that of a savage. When I asked her one day if she had seen the French woman and her children, she said: "Yes, indeed, I have seen her, and I wish that she

[10] Charles Philip LeSueur established a fort above Lake Pepin on the Upper Mississippi in 1695. The exigencies of war with the English led to its abandonment, but in 1700 LeSueur returned to present-day Minnesota to exploit a mine of supposed copper and blue and green earth. The mineral deposits proved worthless, and in 1702 the enterprise was abandoned. For an account of it by a contemporary writer see *Wis. Hist. Colls.*, XVI, 177–93. We have no information about Madam LeSueur apart from that contained in the present memoir.

had never come to this country. I believed
that our women and girls could hold their
own for beauty with those of other nations,
and we even see that those we know are much
inferior to us; but now we know that we are
only monsters compared with your women—
and still we are told that this is not a beautiful woman! Her little children are like the
little Jesuses that Father Gravier shows us
every day."

They are very industrious, being rarely
idle, especially when they are married. In
spring when the nation returns from its winter sojourn, which is at the end of March or
at the beginning of April, they busy themselves gathering wood so as to be able to do
their planting at the beginning of May without interruption, for, although in this country
the snow is not over four fingers deep and
does not lie on the ground a week, and although the rivers are all open at the beginning of March, there are cold spells in May
as severe as those of winter. They spin buffalo hair out of which they make sacks to
keep their peltry in, and of which they also
make garters. They also utilize wood rats
and malodorous animals, whose hides they
color black, red, and yellow. They also work
very well with porcupine quills, with which
they trim their gala moccasins. The Pota-

watomi and Ottawa furnish these to them, for there are no animals of this sort among them. When they wish to finish their sowing early, they offer a feast of flat sides of beef with mixed corn inside of it, and invite as many women as they need to spade up their fields. They do not refuse such invitations, and if any of those invited fail to attend, they come next day to offer their excuses and to tell the reasons which prevented their coming.

At the beginning of June they hill up their corn, and after that the village sets out on the buffalo hunt. Some of the women always remain in each cabin; I have seen times when not six remained. Some days after this they go off in boats, of which they have as many as three in each cabin, to cut reeds with which they cover their cabins. These are a kind that grow in their marshes. They procure bundles of them, which, after removing a skin that encloses several blades conjointly, they dry in the sun and tie together with twine which they make of white wood, with ten or twelve bands at intervals of about six inches. They make these up to ten fathoms in length. They call them *apacoya*, a word which serves not merely to designate these, but which is a generic term for all sorts of coverings. They use the same term for bark boards, and two of these *apacoyas*, one on top of the other, protect one from the rain as well as the best blanket. These are the cabins which they use in autumn and winter; even if they leave their boats the women carry these on their backs.

I have forgotten to say that before they set out for the chase the men play at lacrosse, a few women mingling with them. They make the racket of a stick of walnut about three feet long, which they bend half way, making the end come within a foot of the other end, which serves them for a handle. To keep it in this shape they fasten a buffalo sinew to the curved end, which, as I have already said, they fasten about a foot from the end which serves as a handle. They lace the interior with more buffalo sinew so that the ball, which is a knot of wood of the size of a tennis ball, cannot pass through.

This nation is composed of eight villages, of which there are six at Pimitoui, and two others which I have never seen with them. The latter are situated eight leagues below the mouth of the Illinois River on the Mississippi; they are called Cahokia and Tamaroa, and have, I believe, more than sixty cabins. The six of which I wish to speak are the Kaskaskia, Peoria, Moingwena, Coiracoentanon, Tamaroa, and Tapouara. The Pe-

oria and Coiracoentanon usually join against
the four other villages because they are as
numerous as the four.

In the middle of the prairie on whose edge
their village stands they place two forks
about ten paces apart. An old man who is
neutral rises and utters a cry which signifies:
It is time. Everybody rises and utters cries
similar to those they give when they attack
the enemy. The old man throws the ball into
the air and pell-mell they all try to catch it.
They strike their legs so forcibly that they
are sometimes crippled, especially when someone manages to get the ball in hand so as to
throw it a long way, so that it has sufficient
distance to gain momentum and then strikes
a player's legs in front. This makes them fall
down in such a manner that you might sup-
pose they would never get up again. I have
seen men in this state who were thought to
be dead. The players rush over them without paying any heed; only their female relatives come and carry them off in a deerskin.
Sometimes as much as two months elapse
before they can make use of their legs, and
often they break them.

I have seen a bardash who was standing
aside like the women to send back the ball to
his party, in case it came his way, who was
struck so hard by the ball that his eye was

knocked out of his head. It is necessary to go and return to win the game.

To return to the occupations of the women, at the end of July they begin to mix or dry the corn. They make two kinds. That which they roast gives them more trouble than that which they boil, for they have to make large griddles and take particular care to turn the ears from time to time to prevent their burning too much on one side, and afterwards they have to shell off the kernels. They therefore make very little of this kind. The kind which they boil they gather just as tender as the corn for roasting, and with shells, which they find more convenient than knives, they cut off all the kernels, throwing away the cobs, until they have as much as they wish to cook for that day. They never keep any for the next day because of the excessive care required to prevent it from turning sour. After it has boiled for a few minutes they spread it on reed mats, which they make in the same manner as those that serve for their cabins. The drying process usually takes two days. They make a great store of food of this kind.

After they have gathered the large ears, which are ripe at the end of August, they husk them and spread them on mats. At nightfall they gather them into a heap and cover them well; when the sun is up they spread them again, and they keep this up for a week; then they shell the corn with big sticks six or seven feet long, in a place which they surround with matting to prevent the flying kernels from getting lost. They also harvest a great many fine watermelons. I have seen many of them as big as a water bucket.

They have an abundant supply of fine pumpkins. They have a way of drying them that is not common to all the nations of this region, by which they keep from one year to the next. They scrape the rind well, and take out all the inside, and cut them into circular slices an inch thick. They let them dry for a day in the air, after which they tie them up, putting as many as five pumpkins together in this way. Then they expose them to the sun for several days, which dries them out so thoroughly that they break like a turnip. They cook this with meat and corn. It is a great treat among them. The French always make a liberal stock of this food.

There are also many roots which the women gather. The one which they like best is the *macopine*. This is a big root which they get in the marshes. I have never tried to learn what the flower is like, so I cannot describe it, although I have seen the women pull the roots up from the ground at the bottom of the water, into which they sometimes wade up to the waist, and often duck their heads under the water to pluck them up. Some of them are as big as one's leg. The savages say that they are poisonous when raw, which I hardly believe.

The women have unusual difficulty in cooking them. Sometimes three or four cabins combine and dig a hole in the ground five or six feet deep and ten or twelve square. They throw a lot of wood into it, which they set on fire, and when it is burning briskly they throw in a number of stones which they turn over with big levers until they are red hot. Then they go in quest of a large quantity of grass which they get at the bottom of the water and which they spread over the stones as well as they can to the thickness of about a foot. After this they throw on many buckets of water, and then each cabin puts its roots in its own place as fast as they can, covering them over with dry grass and bark and finally earth. They leave them thus for three days, during which they shrink to half their former size.

In these same marshes they also gather other roots which are as big as one's arm and all full of holes. These give them no trouble to prepare; they merely cut them into pieces half as thick as one's wrist, string them, and hang them in the sun or in the smoke to dry. This root has large leaves that spread out on the water, like the plant we call *votets*, but they are much larger. Between two of these leaves grows an object shaped like the body of a drinking-glass in which are the seeds, which are as big as hazelnuts. They also store up onions as big as Jerusalem artichokes, which they find in the prairies, and which I think are better than all the other roots. They are sugary and pleasing to the palate. They are cooked like the *macopines*.

There are a great many others of which I make no mention whatever, which attests the abundance of everything in this country. Some bits of red copper have been discovered in the vicinity of the river, but up to the present time no mine has been found. We have only found farther down it several lead mines which are very rich. The French and the Indians make use of no others and they even carry on a trade in lead with the Indians who come to trade with them.

There are blackberry bushes here as large as those of France, and the berries are almost as big and as good. No doubt there are sim-ples also, since these savages sometimes cure themselves of wounds for which our surgeons would require six weeks.

There are trees which in autumn have great pods in which there are black stones with a sort of green unguent inside, of which the savages have no knowledge. There is another tree which has branches filled with thorns as long as one's fingers. It also has pods which are not so big nor so long. They are full of little beans which are very hard. There is also found in this pod a gummy substance of a sugary taste, which I was told the English utilize to make punch.

There are remarkably fine Indian chestnut trees, full of nuts bigger and finer than those of Lyons. There is no one who on seeing them does not believe them to be excellent. When we first established this settlement, I went out hunting one day. As I wished to go farther into the woods to shoot more easily at a flock of bustards which I had seen at the water's edge, I advanced and found a quantity of these chestnuts at the foot of the trees. I now thought only of gathering them, and having collected a heap of the finest ones, I was unwilling to leave such a charming spot until I had tasted this fruit. So I made a good fire and put a dozen of them into it which I had taken care to open. When I drew them out of the fire they looked wonderfully inviting. I bit into one thinking I was going to eat the best chestnut in the world, but I was well paid for my curiosity, for I was unable to get rid of the bitterness in my mouth for more than a quarter of an hour. However, I did not regret my failure to shoot the bustards. This game bird is very common here, as well as swans, French ducks, musk ducks, teals, and cranes, both white and gray.

I am now going to relate something which will perhaps not be believed, though I am not the only one who has witnessed it. The waters are sometimes low in autumn so that all the kinds of birds I have just mentioned leave the marshes which are dry, and there is such a vast number of them in the river, and especially in the lake (at the end of which the Illinois are settled on the north shore), on account of the abundance of roots in it, that if they remained on the water, one could not get through in a canoe without pushing them aside with the paddle, and yet the lake is seven leagues long and more than a quarter of a league wide in the broadest part.

This river also has a great abundance of fish, and especially the lake, in which there are carp much better than we have in France, two feet long and half a foot thick. A savage, in good weather, spears as many as sixty of them in a day. There are brills of monstrous size. I have seen one whose eyes were 16 inches apart and whose body was as big as the biggest man. The late Monsieur de Tonty told me that he had seen one with an interval of eighteen inches. I do not doubt that there are some even bigger, for once a soldier of the garrison at that time among the Illinois went fishing one night in a boat, and having put out a big rock to anchor it, hooked one of these brills, which made such a powerful effort to escape that it carried away the canoe, the rock, and the man. The soldier, seeing this, exerted all his strength and was pulling it toward him when the line, which was of whitewood bark, twisted thicker than one's thumb, broke.

While the women are working, from morning till night, as I have already related, the men rest under shelters which the women set up in front of their cabins and cover with foliage to keep the heat of the sun from entering. At night most of the men, seated like dogs on mats of round reeds, play with straws. For markers they use the little beans which I have mentioned, which grow on the thorn trees. The game is usually of 200 straws of the length of a foot. The one who can best deceive is the best player, so they are always on the lookout against being deceived. They mark one or two with their beans, according to the wish of the one whose turn it is to mark, then three, and so in regard to the other players up to six, which is the game. One of them takes the straws in both hands and thrusts his thumb into the middle. The other, if he so desires, does the same thing, and afterwards counts the straws by sixes; if he happens to have one left, and one bean is marked the first, he has the head; if the other gets two which are marked next, it is what they call the neck which comes after the head, so he loses; if he gets one like the other, they begin over again. They have perhaps five or six hundred of these beans, some of which they stake on each play, and when one player has them all before him, they gain what they have staked.

Nothing can exceed their ardor for this game. Some of them have staked their sisters after having lost all they had of personal property. They are very superstitious about it, and if their wives are with child when they lose, they say it is they who bring ill-luck; if they win, they say the contrary. They fear the women and girls when they have the malady to which they are all subject. Because of this, opposite every cabin there is another just large enough to hold two persons, to which they retire with a kettle, a spoon, and a dish during all the time they are in this condition. No one enters save those who are in the same condition. When they need anything they come to the door to ask for it. When it is their first time, they make themselves cabins in the wilderness at a distance of more than ten arpents from the village, and all their relatives advise them to abstain from eating and drinking as long as they are in this condition, telling them that they see the Devil, and that when he has spoken to them they are everlastingly fortunate and achieve the gift of great power for the future.

I saw a young girl of sixteen who was foolish enough to remain six days without eating or drinking and whom it was necessary to carry back to her cabin, after thoroughly washing her of course, because she was not able to stand up. She made all her relatives believe that she had seen a buffalo, which had spoken to her, and that her two brothers who were leading a war party against the Iroquois would make a successful attack without losing anyone. They did indeed make a successful attack, as she had said, but one of the two brothers was killed. All the medicine men said she had been right, because the attack had succeeded, but that apparently she had not fasted long enough, which was the reason the Devil had lied in a part of what he had said to her, since she had performed only a part of what she ought to have done.

The women also cannot be delivered in the cabins of their husbands, but betake themselves to those of which I have just spoken. When they have a painful childbirth, forty or fifty young men make a descent upon the cabin at a time when they are least expected, uttering cries like those they make when they attack their enemies, shooting off guns, and striking heavy blows upon the cabin, which brings about immediate delivery. The women sometimes remain a fortnight, in cases of very difficult childbirth, for although they are savages some of them are quite as sick as our women. Afterwards the woman goes off to bathe; when the water is too cold, she washes in the cabin. On the day when she is to return to her husband's cabin, he has everything cleaned, has his furs shaken, and the ashes in the fireplace removed, so that not a speck remains, after which he kindles a new fire with his fire-drill and lights it himself. Then he sends word to his wife to enter. I have seen some women go to the woods the day after they had borne a child and bring home as heavy a load as usual.

While the women are nursing, their husbands do not ordinarily have commerce with them. As they have several wives, the ab-

stinence is easy for them. They usually
marry sisters and the aunts or nieces of their
wives; they call these *Nirimoua*. When a
man is a good hunter it is very easy for him
to marry all who stand within this degree of
relationship. The women designate him in
the same manner.

When their husbands die, they weep in a
way that would make you think they are
sincerely grieved. In this they are like the
majority of our own women, who weep only
in proportion to the loss they have sustained
and the fear they entertain of not finding new
husbands, and not from the love they bore
the deceased. They abstain for a long time,
as I have already said, from combing themselves unless the sister of the dead man urges
them thereto. Often at daybreak you hear
weeping on all sides, which, however, inspires
laughter rather than pity, for one would say
that they were singing. One calls upon her
brother, another her father, another her
sister, and others their children. She who has
lost her husband and who has no children
names her brother in her funeral song, the
purport of which is that henceforth she will
find no one to do her a good turn.

All the married men have the custom of
giving some present to the brothers of their
wives. The women who have children name

them in their songs, saying that they are deserving of pity in being fatherless, and that they will find nobody who will give them a dress with which to cover themselves. The relatives, of whom all the savages have a great number, come to "clothe" them, bringing them blankets, pelts, kettles, guns, hatchets, porcelain collars, belts, and knives. All that is presented gives pleasure, and now the people of the cabin say that the deceased died opportunely since the esteem in which he was held is shown by these presents from everybody. The next day they simply reverse the process. If some one has given a red blanket, he receives a blue one in return; if he has given a yellow kettle, he receives a red one; if he has given a small kettle, he receives a hatchet, and so on. The only advantage which the relatives of the deceased enjoy is that they often keep good articles for bad ones, which they give away. They also pay four men for burying the dead.

They ordinarily cut two forked sticks ten feet long with a crosspiece. They hollow out the earth to the length of the body and a little wider. They put in a board from one of their old boats or canoes and put the dead body inside with another board on each side.

I forgot to say that they paint his face and hair red, put a white shirt on him if they have one, some new leggings of cloth or of leather, and moccasins, and cover him with the best robe they have. They put in a little kettle or earthen pot, about a double handful of corn, a calumet, a pinch of tobacco, a bow and arrows, and then they replant one of these forked sticks a foot from his feet and the other at the same distance from the head with the crosspiece above, after which they set their stakes archwise on each side, taking care to close up both ends well so that no animals may get in.

If the deceased has been a chief of war parties that have brought in prisoners they plant a tree forty or fifty feet long, which several men go to fetch at the request of the relatives, who give a feast. They peel the bark from this tree and color it with shades of red and black and make pictures of the chief and the prisoners he has taken, tie a bundle of small sticks representing as many persons as he has killed, which they also fasten to the stake, and then they plant it beside the tomb. They sometimes put some articles in the earth, always observing the rule of putting similar things with them in their graves.

After this, so the old men say, they think of procuring for them passage over a great river, on whose nearer shore they hear delightful things. There, they say, there is continual dancing, they have everything they wish to eat, the women are always beautiful, and it is never cold. All the souls of those who die always stand on the bank, waiting to be conveyed to the other side, which never happens unless they have been paid the last obsequies. For this reason the Miami and the Illinois delay as little as possible in rendering them to their relatives. If the deceased is a warrior who has loved the dance, the relatives assemble in his cabin to see what they can give. They count how many villages they represent and agree on the thing as best they can in order that none may be dissatisfied. For this purpose they plant three or four forks, according to the amount of merchandise there is to give, and fix crosspieces on which they hang some kettles, guns, and hatchets. They send word to the chiefs of each village to send their warriors to dance for such a one who is dead in order that he may go to enjoy the bliss which all men will one day enjoy.

Immediately each chief or the leading men of each village exhort the young men to put on their best attire. A large number of mats are spread around outside these forks, and the drummer and the medicine man are close at hand. They seat themselves round about, usually stark naked, and tie the skin of the virile member, sometimes fastening it at the belt. One of them begins his role with war whoops, and they represent in dancing the tableaux presented when they discover the enemy, when they kill him, and when they take his scalp or take him prisoner, and they do all this without losing the cadence. They call this the Discovery Dance. During this time the women are weeping in the dead man's cabin. When the dance is over, the nearest relative of the deceased for whom they dance, pointing with a wand says: This is for you, Peoria; this is for you, Coiracoentanon, and so on. If the deceased liked the game of lacrosse, the relatives have the villages play against each other, and similarly if they liked gaming. Sometimes they have races, and the common people have dances.

When the women die, members of their sex make their graves, dressing them as neatly as they can before burial. If it be a girl, the girls do this. When it happens to be a woman who loved her husband (this is very rare among these women, as it is everywhere else) and he remarries a short time after her death, taking a wife who does not belong to the family of the dead woman, the female relatives invade his cabin and cut up all the skins and break the kettles, while the man never makes a motion. They do the same thing when husbands leave their wives without sufficient reason, and take others of different families.

Although this nation is much given to debauchery, especially the men, the reverend Jesuit fathers, who speak their language perfectly, manage (if one may say so) to impose some check on this by instructing a number of girls in Christianity, who often profit by their teaching and mock at the superstitions of their nation. This often greatly incenses the old men and daily exposes these fathers to ill treatment, and even to being killed. I must say to their glory that they must be saints to take as much trouble as they do for these people. Every day as soon as the sun rises they go into the cabins to find out if anyone is sick; they give them medicines, and if necessary bleed them, and sometimes even make broth for them, after which they have it announced through the village that they are about to say mass. Then they teach the catechism or they preach sermons; in the afternoon, after having applied themselves to the language, they return to the village to hear the catechism, which always takes two hours. The pieces of wood, husks of Indian corn, and even stones which are sometimes thrown at them do not dismay them. They continue their discourse, con-

tenting themselves with saying that it is the
Master of Life who orders them to do what
they are doing, and that those who do not
wish to hear his word may stay away, while
those who wish to listen to it may do so. In
the evening they again call them to prayer,
which is followed by a prayer service for the
French.

No weather prevents them from going
through with the same exercises. Sometimes
they are sent for at night to come to the edge
of the village, which is more than an eighth
of a league long, to assist the dying. I have
even had some differences with some of these
reverend fathers over this matter, on account
of the dangers to which they exposed us in
thus exposing themselves, fearing as I did
that some medicine men, jealous at finding
themselves cut off from what they might
have gained by caring for the sick, might
directly or indirectly do them some mischief.
But their great zeal always carried them
away, no matter what stipulations they made
with me.

This nation, as well as the Miami, has no
religion. Some have the buffalo, the bear,
others the cat, the buck, the lynx, for their
manitou. Almost all the old men are medicine men and consequently healers, so that
when a person is sick the relatives hang a

kettle up in the cabin or a couple of guns, or a blanket, according to the severity of his disease and the amount of his property, after which they send for the one who inspires them with the most confidence and say to him: "Father," or "Brother," or "Uncle," according to the tie of kinship existent between them. (It should be stated that almost all of them call each other relatives, and such degrees of kinship as I have just enumerated are often claimed by persons whom we would not even call cousins. I have seen men of eighty claim that young girls were their mothers.) "I beg of you to take pity on us and heal us. Here is what we had hung up for this."

The old man pretends not to notice what they show him, but approaches the sick man and asks him in what way he is ailing, and where and for how long a time he has been ill. After a thorough inspection, he returns home to get some of his medicine and his *chichicoya*, a gourd from which the inside has been removed and into which they put some glass beads and run a stick through it from the top to the bottom, letting one end project a foot to hold it by. This, when shaken, makes a loud noise. From a little bag in which he has a quantity of small packages he takes out some pieces of tanned skin in which are his medicaments. After spreading them out, he takes up his gourd and shakes it, intoning at the top of his voice a song in which he says: "The buffalo (or the buck, according to his manitou) has revealed this remedy to me and has told me that it was good for such and such a malady"—and he names the one by which the sick man is attacked—"whoever has it administered to him will be healed." Sometimes he reiterates this for half an hour, though often the patient has not slept for a whole week.

When the sickness is a desperate one he calls for water, which he has warmed, and puts into it a *micoine,* mixing with it five or six kinds of powders which he takes from his packages. This he has his patient swallow, then he takes some into his own mouth, and having the place pointed out to him which gives pain, he spouts this drug upon it, and than bandages it. He is careful to make two visits a day and to treat his patient in the same fashion, save that he does not sing unless the sick man is worse.

When he perceives any improvement he brings his gourd and sings louder than the first time, asserting in his song that his manitou is the true manitou, who has never lied to him, wherefore, thanks to the promise which the latter has given him by night in his dreams, he is about to heal his patient by extracting the cause of his ill. Having had the place pointed out, he fingers it carefully, and then all of a sudden throws himself mouth down upon it, crying out as if he were mad. Sometimes he bites his patient so hard as to draw blood, but the latter does not budge for fear of manifesting cowardice. Meanwhile he inserts in his mouth the claw of a dog or an eagle, or the hair of the beard of a Kinousaoueine or a Richion, which he says he has drawn out from the sore spot.

The savages say that it is animals of this kind which send them these diseases because they have eaten their prey. It sometimes happens that they pass by places where such animals have strangled bucks, and if they have no meat, they make no scruple of appropriating and eating them and they even consider this food very good. In spite of all these medicine men say about this they are themselves the first to do it. Then in a long song he thanks his manitou with his *chichicoya* for making it possible for him frequently to obtain merchandise through his favor. He takes his patient out for a bath or washes him in the cabin, according to the season. He takes what had been hung up for him in the cabin and carries it off without saying anything. The relatives rise and pass their hands

over his head and his legs, a sign of profound
gratitude.

Generally they do not cure the sick, although assuredly they have excellent drugs,
because they are ignorant of internal mala-
dies. It is only mere chance when they succeed. The medicines they use for purging
have all the effectiveness possible. There are
some who use coloquinte, with which the
wilderness abounds in autumn, when they
gather their seeds. Some of them are very
skilful in healing wounds. I have seen them
cure some surprising ones in a very short
time. The sucking process which they all
practice has no doubt a large share in this
success. However full of pus a wound may
be, they clean it out entirely without inflict-
ing much pain. They take the precaution of
putting a little powder in their mouths; but
when they have drawn off the worst of it
they no longer do so, but continue to suck at
the wound until it appears ruddy, after which
they chew up some medicine which they spit
upon the wound, merely wrapping up the
whole by day, while leaving the wound to
suppurate. They also wrap it at night.

When a man has been wounded by a gunshot or by an arrow through the body, at the
bottom of the neck or opposite a rib, they
open his side, after taking care to raise the

skin a little so that on being lowered again the opening will be between two ribs. They pour into him a quantity of warm water, in which they have diluted some of their drugs, after which they have the patient make motions and inhale, and sometimes they even grasp him by the arms and legs, pushing him to and fro between them, and then make him eject all this water through his wound, expelling along with it fragments of clotted blood, which otherwise, doubtless, would suffocate him. Then they sprinkle him with some of their powdered herbs, which they put into their mouths, as I have said already, and they never close up the wound by day. I have seen two men who were healed in this way.

As for those who have broken arms or legs, when they manage to get to the village they are healed in less than two months. They do not know what amputation is, as practiced by our surgeons, and we therefore see no savages with one arm or with a wooden leg.

Those who heal such wounds pass for manitous and inspire fear in the young men, and especially in the young girls, whom they often seduce, owing to their weakness in believing that these men might cause their death by blowing medicine upon them, because of which they dare not refuse them.

They also have an extraordinary and ridiculous manner of inspiring belief in the infallibility of their remedies, which, however, has quite the effect they wish on the minds of the young. Two or three times in the summer they plant some poles in the ground in the most attractive spot in their village, forming a sort of enclosure half an arpent square, which they furnish with mats. Meanwhile the medicine men and the medicine women all remain in the cabin of one of their fellows, waiting for all this to be arranged and planning together what to do in order more easily to hoodwink the young people and keep alive the faith in their magical powers, both for the reward which they get for attending to the sick and also with a view to keeping the younger generation under their influence when they wish them to do something for the security of their village or the repose of their wives and children.

After these preliminaries, they enter gravely into this enclosure, their dresses trailing, having their *chichicoya* in their hands and carrying bearskins on their arms. They all sit on mats which are spread for them. One of them rises, the *chichicoya* in his hand, and in a chant addresses the assembly: "My friends, today you must manifest to men the power of our medicine so as to make them understand that they live only as long as we wish." Then they all rise and, shaking the *chichicoya*, chant: "This buffalo has told me this, the bear, the wolf, the buck, the big tail"—each one naming the animal he particularly venerates. Then they sit down again, still shaking the gourd.

Immediately three or four men get up as if possessed, among them some who resemble men who are on the point of dying. Their eyes are convulsed, and they fall prostrate and grow rigid as if they were expiring. Another falls down also, and rises with an eagle's feather in his hand, the barbs of which are reddened and form a figure suggesting that he has been wounded by it, but has been saved from the consequences by his medicines, and wishes to inject it into the body of one of the band. The latter falls to the ground and expels a quantity of blood from his mouth. The medicine men rush to aid him, they tear away the feather which issues an inch out of his mouth, spout medicine all over his body, and then have him carried off with great solemnity to his cabin, where he is treated like one who has been poisoned. They make him swallow a quantity of drugs, and five or six of them, uttering loud yells, lay hold of him and pull him by the arms and legs. They shake him for a long time in this manner without reviving him. Finally he vomits a quantity of water, and at the same moment they throw down a little rattlesnake. A medicine man picks it up and shows it to all the spectators and chants: "Here is the manitou that killed him, but my medicine has restored him to life." All who are present come like people filled with amazement to see the serpent and chant: "Medicine is the science of sciences."

Rattlesnakes abound among them and every year some one is bitten. This troubles them but little since they have an excellent root which softens the swelling as soon as it is applied to the wound, so that by next day the patient is cured. This root is found in the prairies and is shaped like an onion. The stem grows two feet high; the leaves are very narrow and somewhat resemble those of the sumac. It forms large buds in which the seed is lodged. I have made a point of hunting for it in this country, but have never been able to find any. I have been told that they had still another kind, but I have not become acquainted with it.

As regards rattlesnakes, I had an amusing experience one day when I visited the most famous medicine man in the village of the Peoria the evening before a great jugglery was to take place, like the one I have just spoken of. I found him busy putting medicines into packages. As it was summer, he was seated on a sort of scaffold. There was a pile of skins of bears, cats, and bucks, which he pushed back, not so quickly, however, but that I managed to sit down on it. After talking with him awhile, I felt something stirring under me. I paid no attention to it at first, but feeling it move a second time, I asked him what it was. He began to laugh and told me not to be scared as these were rattlesnakes. This startled me, but I took care not to let him see that it did. I asked him to show them to me. He showed me a buckskin which was tied in the middle and which contained the snakes, hardly anything but their heads being visible. He told me that he had extracted their teeth. I had already heard of all this, but had never believed it, so I asked him to let me see them.

He was surprised at my courage, knowing that the French do not like to see animals of this kind. He rubbed his hands with the grass of which I have spoken and we got down. He untied the skins. The women and girls fled when they saw that we were in earnest. I endured the sight of these animals as well as I could, which I should not have done if I had not known that they had no teeth. They hardly stirred as long as he kept his hand on them. He took up one and pressed its neck. The serpent twisted itself about his wrist. He showed me that the snakes no longer had any teeth, and added that he would make use of them next day in the jesting which they were going to carry on —this is the name they give to these juggleries when they speak of them with the French, because the latter protest against them. He said that he would let the snakes run around without fear of being bitten, and that his associates would pick them up in the presence of the young men, who, looking on and not knowing that the teeth had been extracted, would regard them as manitous.

He said we ought not to condemn this as we did, since it was done for a good purpose; it was necessary that the young men should fear the medicine men when they remonstrated with them for the robberies they sometimes committed among themselves and even among the French, for stealing each other's wives, which often caused the death of some one of them, and even for the insults they offered to the Black Robe who kept the young girls from coming to sleep with them. I replied that, if he could prevent all this wickedness without offending God it would be a very good thing, but that they ought to make use of their medicines without saying that it is the buffalo or the bear who has given them and that these beasts are manitous, since it is forbidden to commit one sin in order to prevent another. To this he would not listen, considering only the present advantage. Very few young men busy themselves with sorcery. When one of them does, it is a sign that he lacks courage. Unless he excels in the profession, he is despised.

Besides the animals I have already mentioned as manitous, they also have several birds which they use when they go to war and as to which they cherish much superstition. They use the skins of stone falcons, crows, carrion crows, turtledoves, ducks, swallows, martins, parrots, and many others that I do not name.

Every young man has a little mat made of the round reeds I have mentioned which grow in the marshes. The women dye them black, yellow, and red, and make them three feet long and two feet wide. They fold over one end about a foot in the form of a comb case, in which they put some of these birds of which I have spoken.

They usually prepare to go to war in the month of February. Before starting, it should be noted that in each village there are several chiefs of the young men who control thirty, forty, and sometimes as many as fifty men. At the time I have spoken of they invite them to a feast and tell them that the time is approaching to go in search of men; so it is well to pay homage, according to their custom, to their birds so that these may be favorable. They all answer with a loud Ho! and after eating heartily they all go to get their mats and spread out their birds on a skin stretched in the middle of the cabin and with the *chichicoyas* they sing a whole night, saying: stone falcon, or crow, I pray to you that when I pursue the enemy I may run as fast as you fly, so that I may be admired by my comrades and feared by our enemies. At daybreak they bring back their birds.

When they wish to go to war, one of them, or the one who is their chief, offers them a feast, usually of dog. After all are in place and have observed a long silence the host says: "My comrades, you know that I have wept for a long time; I have not laughed since the time that my brother, father, or uncle died. He was your relative as well as mine, since we are all comrades. If my strength and my courage equalled yours, I believe that I would avenge a relative as brave and as good as he was, but being as feeble as I am, I cannot do better than address myself to you. It is from your arms, my brothers, that I expect vengeance for our brother. The birds that we prayed to a few days ago have assured me of victory. Their protection, along with your courage, should induce us to undertake anything." Then he rises and, going up to each one, passes his hands over his head and over his shoulders. Then all the guests say: "Ho, ho! It is well. We are ready to die: you have only to speak." They thank him, and then depart at night and go about two leagues from the village to sleep.

It is a rule with them never to set out by day when they go in small parties, because, they say, if they went by day they would be discovered before making their attack. Their band does not ordinarily exceed twenty. The youngest, who is always the one who has shared in the fewest raids, carries the kettle and has charge of the cooking and mends the moccasins for all of them, which is no slight task. Accordingly, he hardly ever sleeps at night; but since this is the custom, they always do it amicably. They take the precaution of hiding stores of bacon and flour and some small kettles in two or three places to serve in case they should be pursued by the enemy, so as not to have to stop to hunt for food.

They also mark places for joining each other in case they are obliged to go by several different routes, and in such cases those who arrive first take a little of what they have left, if they need it, and leave their marks, which they never mistake. For this purpose they paint a picture of themselves on the nearest tree. Although several of them have heads of hair that look just alike, their totems identify them. They all have distinctive ones; one, the Buck, another the Buffalo, the Wolf, the Sun, the Earth, the Water, the Woman, the Child, the Girl, or something formed from these names as, Buckfeet, Bear's Head, Woman's Breast, Buffalo Hump, the Eclipsed Moon or Sun, and so forth. So, after painting themselves as I have related, they draw a line above the head, at the end of which they draw a buffalo or its hump, a buck or its feet, the sun or a cloud above it, and so forth. When they approach an enemy, the leader of the party sends out two of the most active warriors a league ahead to reconnoiter the places through which they must pass. If they see smoke or other signs that lead them to believe the enemy is not far off, they report to the chief, who calls a halt.

I have forgotten to say that the commander carries his mat, into which all his men have put their birds, along with a good stock of herbs for healing the wounded. As soon as they stop, the chief takes out the birds and, after offering a short prayer to them, sends out three or four of the bravest and most active warriors to reconnoiter the enemy. If they chance to find but a man or two, they attack them without warning their comrades. If the number is very considerable they return to report, and after thoroughly examining the place where they are to attack them, they invariably wait until morning when the day is beginning to break, and they never fail to paint themselves and to look to their footgear, as a precaution in case they should be obliged to flee.

Two or three of the youngest warriors remain with the baggage in some secluded spot. At a couple of arpents' distance from the enemy they utter the most astonishing yells in order to frighten him, rushing upon him when he takes to flight. In this they triumph, for they know that the enemy cannot run as well as they—I speak of the Iroquois. While running in pursuit they utter the same cry as their birds. If three of them are in pursuit of one man and are in doubt which of them will lay hands on him, the first one who touches him with some missile is the one to whom the prisoner belongs, even if another should lay hands on him first. They then utter several cries to attract the attention of their comrades who are fighting elsewhere, or who are in pursuit of others, who thus learn what they have done.

When they have bound their prisoners and have reassembled, the leader makes a little harangue in which he exhorts his men to thank the spirit for having favored them, and to make every effort to retire quickly from the spot where they are. They usually march for two days and nights without stopping, resting only at their meals. If, as happens very often, their captives are women who cannot march, they break their heads or burn them on the spot. They do this only in extreme cases, as the man who brings a prisoner to the village is more esteemed than the one who kills six men among the enemy. If unhappily some of their own men have been killed, the leader of the band paints himself with mud all along the road and weeps frequently as he marches, and when he reaches the village he is obliged to take presents to the relatives of those that have been killed to pay for their death, and he is expected to go back soon to avenge the slain. If one of his followers is again killed, he has great difficulty in finding men willing to accompany him a third time, which causes him to be hated by the kinsfolk of the dead, unless by dint of presents he finds means (to use their language) to mend their hearts.

To return to their manner of behaving when they return victorious to the village: two men go ahead, and when they are near enough to make themselves heard, they utter cries for as many persons as they have killed, and give their names. Everyone runs out to meet them, and the first to arrive appropriate everything that the warriors carry. Those who are unwilling to part with some weapon or other object which they prize, take care to hide it the day before their arrival; but they are taxed with avarice. As I have said, if some of them have been killed the leader of the party carries some broken bows and arrows in his hand, and those who precede it utter terrible cries saying: "We are dead!" whereupon the women utter terrible howls until it is learned who the dead ones are, after which only the relatives redouble their outcries.

As soon as the news has become known, a prominent man prepares to banquet the warriors, who are invited to enter. When they have arrived in the cabin which has been prepared for them, oil is immediately brought to them in dishes, with which they grease their legs. The one who gives the feast weeps and goes around passing his hands over their heads to make known to them that some of his relatives have been killed by warriors of the nation from which they bring back prisoners, and that they would give him pleasure in killing them. During this time the prisoners are outside the cabin, for it is a rule with them never to admit slaves into their cabins unless they have been granted their lives. The prisoners sing their death song, holding in one hand a stick ten or twelve feet long, filled with feathers from all the kinds of birds the warriors have killed on the road. This is after having them sing at the doors of the cabins of all those who have most recently had relatives killed.

The old men and the leaders of war parties assemble and decide to whom the slaves shall be given. When they have settled this, they lead one of them opposite the door of the cabin of the person to whom they are giving him, and bringing along some merchandise, they enter and say that they are delighted that the young men have brought back some men to replace, if they desire it, those whom the fate of war has taken away. For this offer great thanks are returned. Soon after this the inmates of the cabin assemble and decide what they will do with the prisoner who has been given to them, and whether they wish to give him his life, a thing rarely done among the Illinois. When he is a man, they bring him in and send for the principal men of the village who have brought them the prisoners. They thank them and give them some merchandise. When they want him put to death, they bring him back to the cabin of the most considerable of those who have offered him, giving the captive to them, with a kettle and a hatchet which they have colored red to represent blood. From there he is taken to others, and according to their decision he dies or lives.

When he is condemned to die, it is always by fire. I have never seen any other kind of torment used by this nation. They plant a little tree in the earth, which they make him clasp; they tie his wrists, and burn him with torches of straw or firebrands, sometimes for six hours. When they find his strength is almost spent they unfasten him and cut his thumbs off, after which they let him, if he wishes, run after those who are throwing stones at him, or who are trying to burn him. They even give him sticks which he holds with great difficulty. If he tries to run after anybody, they push him and he falls on his face, at which they hoot. Sometimes he furnishes a whole hour of diversion to these barbarians.

Finally he succumbs under the strain of his torments, and sometimes drops down motionless. The rabble run to get firebrands, which they poke into the most sensitive parts of his body; they drag him over hot embers, which brings him back to life, at which they renew their hooting, as if they had performed some fine exploit. When they are tired of their sport, an old scoundrel cuts his flesh from the top of the nose to the chin and leaves it hanging, which gives him a horrible appearance. In this state they play a thousand tricks on him, and finally stone him or disembowel him. Some drink his blood. Women bring their male children still at the breast and place their feet in his body and wash them with his blood. They eat his heart raw.

There are men and women who might be called cannibals, and who are called man-eaters because they never fail to eat of all those who are put to death in their villages.[11] At nightfall everybody, big and little, knocks loudly with big sticks on the cabins and on

[11] The practice of cannibalism by the Indians of North America is attested by many observers. Commonly, perhaps, it was motivated by some superstition concerning the transference to the victor of qualities possessed by enemies slain or taken captive. At the Chicago Massacre of Aug. 15, 1812 the victors devoured the heart of Captain William Wells. At the Mackinac Massacre of 1763 they feasted on the body of one of the slaughtered Englishmen. See Alexander Henry, *Travels and Adventures*, 104–105.

their scaffolds in order, as they say, to drive away from their village the soul of the man they have killed.

When they go to war among the Pawnee or Quapaw, who are established on the river of the Missouri, almost all the village marches, and even many women accompany them. Thus they take along whole villages. When they are ready to start several young men go about dancing at the doors of all the cabins, one of whom has a drum on his back. They commonly use an earthen pot, which they half fill with water and cover with a buckskin, which they stretch as tight as they can, and they turn the pot upside down from time to time to moisten the skin, which gives it a better tone. A man stands behind it and beats it. Everybody dances round them and each one gives them something. When the women see that they are preparing for this dance, they lead all their dogs away for any of them that they find they kill and feast on.

They always spare the lives of the women and children unless they have lost many of their own people. In that case they sacrifice some to the manes of their dead, throwing them suddenly into the fire to consume the bodies of their slain ones.

This Missouri River, of which I have just spoken, has many tribes along its banks, and there are still more inland. It comes from the west. It is very beautiful and very wide. It empties into the Mississippi eight leagues from the mouth of the Illinois River. Several savages of the tribes that live there who often come to trade among the Illinois, have assured me that it comes from a great lake, which has still another outlet on the other side, which would lead one to believe from their report that it falls into the Western Sea. The Pawnee and Wichita, who live inland along this river, have relations with the Spaniards, from whom they get horses which they sometimes use to hunt the buffalo. Those which they get from the Spaniards are all differently marked on the buttocks with letters. They call them, so I have heard, *Canatis*, having no other special name for them in their language.

These two nations have an abundance of turquoises, looking like our little glass beads. They use them as ornaments hung from their noses and ears, spinning out the beads to the length of a finger with buffalo sinew, afterwards joining the two ends together, at the bottom of which they hang a triangular shaped turquoise of the thickness of about two crowns and not quite as big as a half-franc piece. They call them pendants and esteem them, according to their beauty, of the value of a slave, who in those regions is sometimes worth a hundred francs. Prisoners from these tribes have told us that they traded these turquoises with Europeans, who presumably can only be Spaniards. From some leagues above its mouth, the river is very rapid, and the soil is so loose that in spring, when the water is high, it is carried off in such great quantity that it renders the Mississippi turbid for more than 200 leagues. The savages of whom I have spoken who come to trade among the Illinois are the Osage and Missouri, who not long ago waged war with them, and who, aside from their need of hatchets, knives, and awls, and other necessary things, are very glad to keep on the good side of this nation, which is much more war-like than theirs. They never fail every year to visit them and to bring them the calumet, which is the symbol of peace among all the nations of the south.

I think I should tell in detail how they proceed when they wish to sing the calumet to some nations. When they are within two leagues of the village to which they are going they send ahead some of their best known people to announce their arrival, how many they are, and to whom they are coming to sing the calumet. Messengers are sent back to them with orders to tell them how

many men are to lodge at the village of the
Peoria, how many at that of the Kaskaskia,
and so on, and whether the one to whom
these strangers have the intention of giving
the calumet is in condition to receive it; for,
boastful as these savages are, they are not
ashamed to confess when they are poverty-
stricken and to designate a proper person to
whom to sing the calumet.

Good cheer is not lacking on their arrival,
and later in the same evening they go off to
the cabin of the one to whom they are to give
the calumet and sing until dawn. They do
this four nights in succession, after which
they make scaffolds outside if it is fine weather
and go in search of the man or of his wives to
whom they sing the calumet. They take him
up on this scaffold and all place themselves
beside him and beat drums and shake their
gourd rattles and sing all day long. Two of
them push him gently to and fro between
them as a still more significant mark of the
honor they do him. Meanwhile everybody
comes to knock at a post, which has been
planted for this purpose, to recite his exploits,
and afterwards they give gifts according to
the ability of each one and in accordance with
the honor deserved by the one to whom they
sing the calumet and the esteem in which
they hold him.

I should have said that this calumet is made like a hatchet, of a red stone that is found toward the Sioux country. It has a very long handle, from which are hung several feathers painted red, yellow, and black, brought together in the form of a fan. This handle is moreover covered with the skins of ducks' necks. During the whole time consumed by the singing, one of them holds the calumet, which he shakes continually before the one to whom it is given. When they see that no more people are coming to strike the post, they cease to sing. They then escort their chief to his cabin and leave him the calumet and several skins of beavers, bucks, or cats. Those who accompany him sometimes receive a load of merchandise when they return. This compliment gives pleasure to the Illinois, and they exult to see strangers come to recognize some of their people as chiefs.

During four consecutive years that I lived with the Wea at Chicago, which is the most considerable village of the Miami, who have been settled there for ten or twelve years, I found no difference between their customs and language and those of the Illinois.[12] The only difference is that they re-

[12] The Wea, or Ouiatanon, were one division of the Miami tribe. When the French first encountered them

main settled in one place only a very short
time.

The year that I first came from France,
they were settled on this side of the old fort.
A year later they separated, part to go to the
upper Mississippi, and the others to the St.
Joseph River and to the mouth of the Root
River which empties into Lake Michigan,
twenty leagues north of Chicago. Both of
the latter and those who went to the Missis-

they were living in the vicinity of Green Bay. About
1668-69 Perrot found them established on the upper Fox
River (of Wisconsin). Apparently, however, the tribe
was widely scattered, and those Indians first encountered
by the French were its northern extension. They re-
sponded to La Salle's call to settle around Starved Rock,
where, as Liette reports, they were living when he came
to the country in 1687. In or about 1690 a Miami village
was established on the main Chicago River, in the heart
of the present business district, and another a mile or
two distant up the South Branch. For an account of
these villages see M. M. Quaife, *Lake Michigan*, Chap. 5.
As early as 1679 La Salle found the Miami settled on the
lower St. Joseph, and their name was given by him both
to the river and to the fort which he built at its mouth,
in present-day St. Joseph, Michigan. Other branches of
the tribe soon became seated on the Wabash (vicinity of
Lafayette, Indiana) and at its headwaters (present-day
Fort Wayne), where their name became permanently
attached to the Maumee, the largest river emptying into
any of the Great Lakes. They were long hostile to the
Americans, but were conquered by General Wayne in
1793-95, and utterly broken by the American armies in
the War of 1812.

sippi remained but a very short time, when they left to establish a village at the Grand Calumet, which also empties into this lake twelve leagues south of Chicago, and another at the fork of the Kankakee River. Three years later part of them removed to the banks of the Wabash, where they still remained when I came down to Canada in obedience to the orders which Monsieur the Marquis de Vaudreuil had sent me. Those who went to the St. Joseph River remained there until Monsieur de la Mothe invited them to come nearer to the Strait. This nation was not useless to us at the time when we had war with the Iroquois. This is especially true of those on the St. Joseph River, owing to the frequency with which war parties of these savages went among them, who rarely returned without making a successful attack.

This nation, I believe, is as populous as the Illinois. It is composed of six villages which are the Chachakingoya, Aouciatenons, Anghichia, formerly Marineoueia, Kiratikas, Minghakokias, and Pepikokia; they are better beaver hunters than the Illinois, and they esteem the beaver more highly.

The Wabash River,[13] of which I have just

[13] For some time after their entry into the western country the French confused the Wabash River with the Ohio. This confusion is reflected in Liette's state-

spoken, on which part of the Miami are settled, is a very beautiful river, and all the savages call it such. I do not know where it has
its source, but I know that it is not very far
from the Iroquois country. It flows contin-
uously southwest and empties into the Mississippi sixty leagues from the mouth of the
Illinois River. It is wider than the Mississippi. The late Monsieur de Juchereau located his fort two leagues within the country.
From the village of the Illinois you travel
southward by land a distance of 60 leagues in
order to get there. It is the most beautiful
country in the world as regards soil. We begin to see here those reeds which serve instead of canes and which shoot up to a height
of fifteen feet. On the other side of the river
there are no more prairies. The woods which
grow on its banks are mostly made up of
those fruit trees of which I have spoken; the
rest are whitewood, walnut, chestnuts, some

ments, which obviously apply to the latter river. To
check the entrance of the English into the Mississippi
country, coming by way of the Tennessee and Ohio
rivers, Iberville commissioned Charles Juchereau de St.
Denis to establish a post at the mouth of the Ohio. This
was done in 1702, but disaster, in the shape of an epi-
demic, soon overwhelmed the colony and the survivors
migrated down river to the settlement on Mobile Bay,
which marks the first settlement of Louisiana. See C.
W. Alvord, *The Illinois Country*, 1673-1818, 133-34.

ash, Norway maples, and hardwood trees. All these varieties of trees attest the fertility of these lands. Spring arrives here a month earlier than among the Illinois. At most there are never more than two inches of snow, which disappears in two days. Although I have been there only in summer, I can speak authoritatively owing to the knowledge which I have got from the Illinois, most of whom go there every year to hunt.

I forgot to say, in the place where I talked of war, that the Illinois as well as the Miami have the rule when small war parties are invading the enemy, never to make more than one fire, fairly long, so that all the warriors may enjoy it. They always lie down with their feet to the fire, and never put anything on themselves. Those of the band who have seen the least of war are assigned to serve the rest. They circulate about the fire, and never unload their packs from their backs to make water, or for any other necessities, and never when going toward the enemy. When they are returning home they unload, but they never sit down on their pack. Nor do they ever make use of knives when their meat is cooked, a thing they do not observe when they make general marches, believing that no one can resist them, in which they are often mistaken.

Memoir of Liette

I desire with all my heart, Monsieur, that this memorial may give you pleasure, and prove worthy of your curiosity.

Montreal, Canada, October 20, 1721.

Signed: DE GANNES